Praise for
DECIDE: The Ultimate Success Trigger

Jim Palmer did it again! Another AMAZING book by a guy who all entrepreneurs should learn from. If you're ready to achieve more success and happiness, then follow the strategies in this brilliant book by my friend, Jim Palmer!

– James Malinchak
Featured on ABC's Hit TV Show, "Secret Millionaire"
Author, *Millionaire Success Secrets*
The World's #1 Big Money Speaker® Trainer & Coach
Founder, www.BigMoneySpeaker.com

If you think this is another feel-good, touchy-feely, self-growth guide – you're mistaken! When I first picked up this book I thought it will be a re-hash of what I already know and I'll quickly put it down. I was wrong! Jim's transparent personal stories, real-life examples, step-by-step advice, and bold calls to action turn *DECIDE: The Ultimate Success Trigger* into the every entrepreneur's ultimate success guide. Franky, I think you'll be making a mistake if you don't buy it and don't read it as quickly as you can!

– Adam Urbanski
The Millionaire Marketing Mentor®
Founder & CEO
TheMarketingMentors.com

Without a doubt, the root cause of what prevents far too many entrepreneurs from achieving their dreams and reaching their fullest potential, is indecision. When opportunities arise or when challenges present themselves, which they always do, the ability to make fast, sound decisions moves businesses forward and helps you grow. I've been studying and teaching on the power of mindset for many years and I must say that Jim Palmer has nailed it with his latest book, *DECIDE: The Ultimate Success Trigger*. I especially appreciate how much Jim shared his own personal demons and struggles and how he overcame them. You will be inspired by Jim's story and moved into action from his strategies.

– Lee Milteer
Author of *Reclaim the Magic* and
Success Is an Inside Job
www.milteer.com

When someone finds out I'm a #1 best-selling author, they say, "I've thought about writing a book." When someone discovers I own three businesses, they say, "I've thought about starting a business." When someone figures out I have online coaching programs, they say, "I've thought about…"

These people live at 1313 I'veThoughtAboutIt Lane, Squishyville, USA.

To all of these people still thinking about it, my friend and hero Jim Palmer says, "DECIDE!" I only wish he had written this book 15 years ago when I was starting out. I would have more hair on my head and money in my accounts.

Read this book as if your business and life depend on it …because they do.

– Dr. Joey Faucette
www.GetPositive.Today

Your ability to make decisions will directly affect your ability to be successful. Should you take retirement funds and start a new company? Should you hire someone to do a task for you or do it yourself? Should you wait or move ahead? Every decision has some knowledge built within it, but in the final analysis, every decision requires a step (or leap) of faith. Jim's new book, *DECIDE: The Ultimate Success Trigger*, is a roadmap to help you learn how to make decisions more efficiently and more timely. I hope you will take time to study each section of this book and then assimilate them into your own life. After all, "you get to choose."

– Steve Graves, Sr.
Chief Fun Officer
Play-a-Round Golf
www.playaroundgolf.net

I've had the privilege of knowing Jim Palmer for many years, and he is an extraordinary coach, entrepreneur and friend. I've read his other books, but *DECIDE* is my favorite by far. I felt like I was sitting side-by-side with Jim in a coaching session as he candidly shares what it takes to be truly successful.

What I like most about this book is Jim's authenticity, transparency and true love for those he currently coaches and those who will be coached by reading this book. If there is anyone that can help you build your dream life, Jim Palmer is the right guy to do it!

– Michelle Prince
Ziglar Certified Speaker / America's Productivity Coach
Best-Selling Author & Self Publishing Expert
www.MichellePrince.com

After reading *DECIDE*, I have DECIDED that this is one of the best tools an entrepreneur can own. I felt that Jim really understood the mental struggles EVERY entrepreneur goes through and gave sound credible advice on the head trash we all deal with. He is right on target with his wisdom and observations. This is definitely a book you should start your entrepreneurial life with and live by it. Thanks Jim for not being afraid to stand tall and tell it all.

– Dr. Raynette C. Ilg N.D.
Naturopath • Author • Speaker
Olive Branch Wellness Center

Jim Palmer's book, *DECIDE,* is amazing! The valuable nuggets of information on clearing head trash, acting and moving forward are a must for every entrepreneur.

– Cindy McLane

Founder, www.TranscribeYourBook.com

As a founder of several multi-million dollar businesses, I've had my share of successes over the past 14 years. They've afforded my family and me the opportunity to live a life I never could have imagined. None of these successes would have been possible had I not decided to take action, even in the face of fear, uncertainty and doubt. When I'm asked the question, "What's your secret to success?" I usually reply by saying "There is no secret." However, after reading this book, I've found I owe much of my success to the very same principles that Jim shares within these pages. Read this book and apply its concepts. I can think of no better manual for the entrepreneurial mind.

– Bobby Deraco

Founder and CEO, Synapse

www.synapseresults.com

Inc. 500 Honoree

Not only did I have the privilege of being featured in Jim's book *DECIDE,* I have the benefit of having Jim as my business coach and reading *DECIDE* was like being in a massive coaching session with him. In *DECIDE,* Jim offers tough love and actionable steps, coupled with a willingness to share the nitty-gritty of what it takes to truly succeed. He articulates not only the barriers, but the essential need for us to *DECIDE* in the midst of fear and uncertainty. Jim's conversational guidance and authenticity makes you feel like he is coming along side you, and rooting for your success. Jim's knows our struggles, he is in the trenches and *DECIDE* is a handbook of wisdom every entrepreneur needs.

– Susie Miller
The *Better* Relationship Coach
www.susiemiller.com

Being an entrepreneur is not an easy road and very few books tell it like it is. Jim Palmer's *DECIDE: The Ultimate Success Trigger* is a warrior's journey at its very best! Arm yourself with real entrepreneurs baring it all about overcoming and beating the odds; turning failure into strength, and mistakes into lessons. Get a highlighter. *DECIDE* is THE guidebook for the journey ahead.

– Brad Szollose
Global Business Adviser
21st Century Workforce Culture Strategist

I read every word. Good information, only wish I had read this book 30+ years ago when I began my selling career. Your personal life struggles are a testimony to the successes that have brought you through to make *DECIDE* a must-read book for anyone asking the hard questions. For those who've ever found themselves face to face, having that 3:00 a.m. moment of self discovery, your book's words help to understand what life is about and how to overcome the many obstacles we ALL face. Thank you for sharing.

– Mark D. Gleason
Author, Entrepreneur, Realtor, Sales Trainer
www.Soldbygleason.com

It's so easy, as an entrepreneur, to get caught up in the head trash that attacks all of us. We think too small and convince ourselves that working harder will result in success. In reality that just isn't true – you end up working harder, don't have time for your family, and are tired all the time. (I know because I've been there!) When you couple that with a fear of success, you have a recipe for getting mired in "Squishyville." This is not a good place to spend your time!

Jim Palmer's book, *DECIDE*, quickly dispels the myths we carry around in our heads and helps us to see beyond whatever ideas that come from our childhood. I can truly say that Jim's books, coaching program, and mastermind group have made a significant difference in myself and my business. I am now empowered to become the successful entrepreneur that I was created to be!

– Diane Gardner
Your Tax Coach
www.taxcoach4you.com

I have read each of Jim Palmer's books, but *DECIDE* is in a class all but itself. This is the best down to earth, real and solid business advice book you must read. Starting in the foreword with the statement "The quality of your choices shapes the quality of your results" to the final question on the very last page of the book "If not now, when?" Each page contains at least one golden nugget, and Jim's advice is always on target and exactly what I need to hear to achieve better results. Get this book now and watch the results you will get if you just follow Jim's advice. The book is the best investment that you can make in yourself and your business right now.

– Nile Nickel
www.LinkedInFocus.com

Jim's book, *DECIDE: The Ultimate Success Trigger*, is by far one of the best books for both new and well-seasoned entrepreneurs. There are many reasons to read this book, but the biggest reason is this: it is not simply a book of suggestions, tips and strategies. Jim opens up and shares details of his personal journey and the many struggles he faced, and how he overcame them to grow his Dream

Business. After reading *DECIDE*, you will feel motivated and inspired into action.

Jim Palmer is the go-to coach for entrepreneurs who are ready to get down to business, toss the excuses and get it done! Give him 30 minutes and he will give you gold (as long as you are willing to put it into action). I highly recommend partnering with Jim to take your business to the next level-fast!

– Kelly Roach
Business Growth Strategist
www.KellyRoachCoaching.com

The Ultimate Success Trigger indeed! In his new book, Jim has really hit the nail on the head with what it takes to succeed as an entrepreneur! Many would-be entrepreneurs fail to realize how vitally important your mindset is to succeeding at ANY endeavor. What you tell yourself, your self-talk will ultimately make or break you. Your success is not determined just by the mechanics of whatever business you are in, but how you make decisions and take action. In *DECIDE*, Jim did not just create another mindset book, but Jim brings key success concepts into clarity by really opening up and sharing his personal experiences; his own journey from struggle to abounding success. Jim shares his success not only in his own business, but also by helping others to achieve abundant success in their own right through his various publications, coaching programs, and events.

Jim is the real deal! *DECIDE* to not just read, but absorb the lessons Jim shares in his book. When you embrace the lessons of *DECIDE*, you will be uncomfortable for a time, but you will not regret it!

– Roy Adler
The Freedom Eagle Blogger.com

During these times, who wouldn't want to "build a more profitable business faster"? Jim's thought-provoking, stimulating and practical book walks you through the exact steps you can take to move you into decision-making mode! I promise you, if you decide to read this book, it might rattle you, get you going, make you really think, but in the end you won't regret taking the time to *DECIDE*! Great read Jim, thanks for helping to equip entrepreneurs!

– Shawn K. Manaher
Sidepreneurs
http://sidepreneurs.com

Just about every entrepreneur will experience a "crisis point" during their journey toward ultimate success. This can be so debilitating, you find yourself a spectator to your own business's impending doom. When this happens, read Chapter 8, "Decide to Use GPS" - and allow Jim Palmer's new success map to guide you toward a more profound success, profitability, and prosperity.

– Adam Hommey
Host, Business Creators' Radio Show
BusinessCreatorsRadioShow.com

Wow! Absolutely love Jim Palmers most recent book *DECIDE*. It's packed full of honest, relevant, and cutting edge tips, tools and strategies for not only overcoming the mental blocks we have as entrepreneurs, but also provides proven techniques for gaining clarity and confidence in making powerful decisions. If you are an entrepreneur who is serious about success and making a difference in the lives of those you touch, this book is for you.

– Travis Greenlee
Master Business Growth Strategist
Profit Groove Marketing – Founder and CEO
www.ProfitGrooveMarketing.com

Working alongside Jim Palmer for over five years I've been privileged to witness a ton of great things from the man himself. As a member of his "Dream Team," I see firsthand exactly what it takes to be successful as an entrepreneur. I've also watched him help many, many people move past their own self-imposed road blocks, quite often in an amazingly short amount of time. In his book, *DECIDE: The Ultimate Success Trigger*, Jim pulls back the veil on the sometimes ugly bits that a lot of entrepreneurs face at some point. This book helps you look in the mirror, face your fears and finally do what you know you need to do, what you've been fighting against all along. Reading this book, and reflecting, I'm very familiar with "Squishyville," I lived there a long, long time - I suppose we all have at some point. Thank you Jim for writing it all down and help to make sense of it all!

– Kate Bradbury
Admin Icons, Inc.
kate@adminicons.com

There are a ton of business books available for entrepreneurs to read and use as they work on growing their businesses. *DECIDE* stands apart from the rest because of Jim's authenticity and straightforward style of coaching. The whole book is fantastic, but for me, just one chapter gave me the motivation to decide to raise my prices and by doing that, my revenue grew immediately. I can only imagine how much my business will grow as I continue to implement the advice written throughout DECIDE!

– Jessica Rhodes
Founder of InterviewConnections.com

I thought the *Stop Waiting For It to Get Easier* book was the blueprint for my business, but after reading *DECIDE*, all I can say is WOW!!! This is truly a life changer and contains some of the juiciest insights into what really makes the difference between a successful and unsuccessful entrepreneur. High-level business lessons cloaked in colorful, entertaining and insightful story telling. This is a must read for anyone looking to take their business to the next level.

– Gary George
Blazin Multimedia
www.blazinmultimedia.com

Do you know a friend, colleague, or perhaps a group
that would enjoy and benefit from the information and
strategies in this book?
If so, we're happy to extend the following volume discounts!

DECIDE
The Ultimate Success Trigger

$19.95 U.S.

Special Quantity Discounts
5-20 Books - $16.95
21-50 Books - $13.95
51-100 Books - $11.95
101-250 Books - $8.95
251-500 Books - $6.95

Call or e-mail today to order bulk quantities

DECIDE:
The Ultimate Success Trigger

By Jim Palmer

Your Dream Business Coach

With a Foreword by

Melanie Benson Strick

America's Leading Small Business Optimizer

Dream Business Coaching

Dream Business Academy

DECIDE: The Ultimate Success Trigger

Published by Success Advantage Publishing
64 East Uwchlan Ave.
P.O. Box 231
Exton, PA 19341

ISBN: 978-0692396681

Cover design by Jim Saurbaugh, JS Graphic Design

DISCLAIMER AND/OR LEGAL NOTICES

This book is dedicated to my family,
Stephanie, Nick, Steve, Jessica, and Amanda.

Table of Contents

Foreword

There are a few concepts that can transform you from the inside out. One of those is a principle that I learned many years ago that I use daily in my own journey: "The quality of your choices shapes the quality of your results."

For the first 18 months of my career as an entrepreneur, I struggled financially. Working 14-hour days, it seemed that I could work another four hours a day and still not achieve the dream. One day I realized that the biggest impediment to my cash flow was me. I was not making the best decisions on how to grow my business. My mindset was influencing every decision I made in a negative way – and I was rationalizing all my poor choices because my deep belief was that I was not capable of being successful.

In a pivotal moment, I knew I needed to make a new choice. Instead of struggling, I decided to be the person who could easily have a six-figure business. Whatever action I needed to take, behavior I needed to have, or thought pattern I needed to shift... I was willing.

Nine months later I broke six figures for the first time, and I've never looked back.

I've been mentoring thought leaders and creative, visionary entrepreneurs for over 14 years now, and I've come to realize there's one factor that holds true: Each decision you make is either moving you closer to your ultimate goal of success or is putting you on the path of distraction, causing you to become derailed and focused on activities that cannot deliver you to the gold.

Anyone who has ever started a business knows that one decision can change everything in life. The decision to start a business can mean freedom! No more bosses and all the independence you could ever want. Once you make that decision to be an entrepreneur, making the best decisions possible is a muscle you must strengthen. Entrepreneurs are faced with daily decisions like...

How much should I charge?

What should I do to market my offering so that people will buy it?

Who will be the best assistant I could hire to help me get everything done?

Which of these ten opportunities will actually generate the best leads without wasting my time?

What task should I do next?

Should I pick up that phone call or let it roll to voice mail?

As a matter of fact, you'll find that strengthening your core "decision-making" muscle to make excellent decisions is essential. Today we are barraged with so much information that making good decisions can become overwhelming. Between all the email, social media, text messages, phone calls, Google Hangouts, daily webinars, and even workshops and live trainings, there is no shortage of information bombarding us.

How we use our time has never been more complex. We stretch our brains trying to do it all and keep up with an ever growing list of action items.

But, and many people don't quite realize this, you cannot make good decisions when your brain is full of fear, stress, and problems. An entrepreneur who is spinning in overwhelm has a diminished capacity to think strategically and clearly.

Here's an interesting fact: The mind can only process five to seven bytes of information at one time. And, as I previously mentioned, there's at least a billion bytes of information trying to get our attention. Your ability to quickly parse that information and make decisions is crucial to achieving higher levels of success without overwhelm and stress.

Your ability to rise above the noise of life and create space for clear decision making will serve you well. That's why Jim Palmer's book, *DECIDE: The Ultimate Success Trigger*, is one of the best books you will ever read. Within these pages lies the wisdom of not just one successful entrepreneur but two wise souls... and even more. Jim has shared my own success principles alongside his extraordinary guidance – you are literally gaining insight into two of the best business minds in the industry. Plus he has included additional insights from members of his Dream Business Mastermind and Coaching Program.

Jim and I have been a part of each other's success journey for many years. First, Jim was a member of one of my coaching programs. Then we partnered to create MARS (Magnetic Attraction and Retention Program) together. We immediately saw how the synergy between our two styles could bring great value to the community of entrepreneurs we serve. Now we are in a mastermind and have become life-long friends.

There's nothing more valuable as an entrepreneur than being in regular connection with movers and shakers who challenge you to be the best you can be. I'm beyond fortunate to have that kind of mutual support with Jim. That's why when he asked if he could share a few of my coaching principles in his book I said, "Yes! Absolutely!"

Read this book first to get the overall principles. Then read it again with a highlighter and pen to take notes. You couldn't get better coaching unless you hired one of us directly. Make this book your best friend and come back to it over and over again. You'll find that each time you read it, you'll uncover a different nugget of wisdom – exactly when you need it the most.

Melanie Benson Strick
America's Leading Small Business Optimizer
www.MelanieBensonStrick.com

Foreword

Preface

If you are an entrepreneur, wanntrapreneur (someone wanting to start a business), sidepreneur (someone who has small business on the side while still holding a job – a term I first heard when Shawn Manaher interviewed me for his radio show by the same name), or a small business owner seeking higher growth and profitability, this book is written for you. It will help you build a more profitable business faster.

DECIDE will prove to be *Your* **Ultimate Success Trigger!**

My recommendation is to move this book to the top of your to-be-read pile of books (I know you have one) and start reading immediately. Why the urgency? Because none of the skills and talents you already possess and none of the marketing strategies you may soon employ are going to help you build your Dream Business until and unless you unleash the Ultimate Success Trigger. It is *that* powerful.

DECIDE is one of the most important books I've written so far and will prove to be the most important book you'll read along your entrepreneurial journey.

I published *Stop Waiting for It to Get Easier – Create Your Dream Business Now* in October 2013. At that point, I had written five books in five years, and to be candid, I wasn't sure if I wanted to write another one! Writing a book requires an enormous amount of time, dedication, and energy, and with the growing demand for my coaching services and running two live events each year (Dream Business Academy), I felt like I needed a break from writing.

But that all changed when I began feeling the "nudges."

In March 2014 at my sold-out Dream Business Academy in Las Vegas, I taught a module titled, **"Success – Mindset and Money,"** and the audience loved it. Candidly, they liked it more than I thought they would! In this module, I share a lot of my entrepreneurial journey, particularly as it relates to my mindset about success, money, debt, and the hundreds of decisions I made in the early, lean years of my business.

My commitment to the entrepreneurs and small business owners who attend Dream Business Academy is be transparent and pull back the curtain on how I built my Dream Business and how I continue to market and grow it today. It is one thing to attend an event where you hear the latest technology or strategy that's working today, but I felt that sharing the early struggles, mistakes, and not so glamorous details of building a business would be also instructive and beneficial.

Reliving some of my struggles, challenges and personal demons with a live audience is not easy, but when I saw some entrepreneurs with tears in their eyes, I knew I was hitting close to home. I also knew then that my challenges were not unique: in many ways, my story was their story. Sharing it was helpful to both them and me.

That was my first nudge.

In September 2014 at my Dream Business Academy in Philadelphia, I taught this module again, and when I finished, some of the entrepreneurs suggested that I write a book on the subject of mindset, focusing on how it relates to the hundreds of decisions and choices new entrepreneurs make when starting and building their businesses.

Another nudge.

On the next break, a few more attendees approached me and shared privately that what I revealed about my journey touched them deeply and, in some cases, gave them the courage and encouragement they needed to push through their current struggle – to keep on "keeping on." Wow.

After the event, an entrepreneur who I respect and admire said, "Jim, I believe that you need to share your story with a larger audience because entrepreneurs need to hear it. Especially during this difficult economy, many entrepreneurs are struggling, and instead of the usual "cheerleader" speech, hearing what you faced and how you overcame it to build your business would be very beneficial and inspiring."

BAM! Another nudge.

The Decision! Promoting and running a live event takes a great deal of energy, and I always schedule a few days off afterward to decompress and recharge. Following the Philadelphia event, I spent a couple days on my boat staring out at the beautiful Chesapeake Bay... thinking about the powerful experience and yes, the nudges.

I've learned somewhat late in life not to ignore the nudges, so while sitting on my boat, I made a commitment to write the book you're now holding. Yes, I DECIDED to forgo my initial thoughts about taking a break from book writing and write *DECIDE*.

Today I run several businesses, but one of my greatest joys is helping other entrepreneurs start and grow profitable businesses. I do this largely through my Dream Business Mastermind and Coaching Program (I'll include some information on this unique program in the back of this book and you can also learn more at www.DreamBizCoaching.com), but with this book, I'll be able to help even more entrepreneurs and small business owners take their businesses to the next level.

NOTE: This is not simply another "mindset" book!

This book is about the importance and business-building power that comes when you have the ability to DECIDE. It's about the hundreds of choices we make as entrepreneurs, and it's about challenging you to do the one thing that I've learned through six years of coaching is actually quite difficult for many entrepreneurs – deciding, making a decision – yes or no, but not maybe!

Deciding one way or the other and moving forward. Deciding and moving forward, and taking corrective action if necessary, is one of the main traits that separates ordinary entrepreneurs from highly successful entrepreneurs. Deciding is the one thing that can trigger success like nothing else.

Confidence comes from success, and success comes from moving forward. And moving forward faster comes from the ability (and confidence) to make fast decisions and implement them.

Think of this book as a private conversation or coaching session between the two of us. You'll find it no-nonsense and hard hitting and as always, you can count on me to candid and blunt with my suggestions and recommendations. You can also count on me to share some straight talk about what it takes to achieve significant success as an entrepreneur... to grow your Dream Business and create the dream lifestyle you want and deserve.

Unlike speaking to an audience, where you get instant feedback, writing a book often leaves you wondering – is this information resonating? So, if this book helps you in a small or large way, I would be grateful if you let me know! You can post a comment on my Facebook page, or if you prefer to remain anonymous, please email me at guru@thenewsletterguru.com – I'd love to hear from you!

God bless you and I hope *DECIDE* will soon be Your Ultimate Success Trigger.

Acknowledgements

As always I thank God for saving my life. After facing what I describe as my "season of crisis" – 15 months of devastating unemployment, debt, shattered confidence, and just for good measure, Stage II cancer – God rescued me and my life has been simply extraordinary and blessed ever since.

I thank Stephanie for being my wife, my greatest supporter, and best friend of 34 years. She is an amazingly patient person and more than anyone has taught me the importance of serving others. I truly cannot imagine my life without her.

My four children, Nick, Steve, Jessica, and Amanda, have all moved on and in most cases, away! But even from a distance, they continue to cheer me on, and I'm very proud of the adults they have become.

As I mentioned in my last book, one of the greatest joys in the last few years has been helping Jessica start her home-based business, so she can be a stay-at-home mom to Nathan. She is doing phenomenally well.

Last but most certainly not least, I want to thank my grandson, Nathan, for helping me stay young and a kid at heart. Thanks to FaceTime and Skype video, I get to visit with Nathan frequently, and when Nathan visits, I forget everything else and get down and play with him, read with him, and I've even taught him some Creedence Clearwater on guitar. Nathan loves driving my boat and is an Eagles fan. What grandfather could ask for more!

The amazing growth of my business would not be possible without my incredible support team – my Dream Team! Thank you to my remarkable personal assistant, client service manager and friend, Kate; the Sensei of my web presence, Adam; my lead designer, Chris; my interview scheduler, head of Pinterest marketing, and so many other things, Jessica; amazing client support rep and Concierge lead designer, Lyndsay for providing outstanding client support to our hundreds of valued clients; Amy for the hundreds of "Newsletter Guru" and "Dream Business" graphics that make me look so good; Julie-Ann, Helen, and Matt for leading my team of content writers; Mike and his team at Mikel Mailings for printing and mailing my monthly No Hassle membership programs; Bobby, Jacki, and the entire team at Synapse for being outstanding partners in my Concierge Print and Mail on Demand program; and thank you to Ann Deiterich for doing a wonderful job editing this book. Ann has been a part of all my books, and she's done an incredible job taking both my written words and my thoughts and making me sound a lot smarter than I am!

To Your Success,

Jim Palmer

Chapter One:
Nothing Happens in
Squishyville

Every day, if not every hour, entrepreneurs are faced with a never-ending array of choices. When a decision needs to be made, you essentially have three options: "yes," "no," or "I'll think about it." The last option leads directly to Squishyville.

It is my strong belief that deciding "yes" or "no" moves your business forward at a much faster rate of speed than postponing the decision. Your ability to **DECIDE** *is* **the Ultimate Success Trigger**.

As an entrepreneur, your ability to get more comfortable accepting and managing risk and making faster decisions will help you grow a more profitable and successful business in less time.

A quick word about the title, *DECIDE - The Ultimate Success Trigger*:

As I mentioned in the Preface, I made the decision to write this book while relaxing on my boat last September after my Dream Business Academy in Philadelphia. My first thoughts, based on input from the attendees of Dream Business Academy, were that this was not going to be a mindset book. I didn't necessarily disagree with the importance of mindset; however, there were and are already a plethora of books on success and entrepreneurial mindset.

From the granddaddy of them all, *Think and Grow Rich* by Napoleon Hill to countless other books with futuristic-looking pictures of the human brain with firing synapses on the cover, there is no shortage of mindset books.

My goal was to not be "another mindset book" and get caught in the clutter and noise of that crowded arena.

One of the marketing strategies I teach my coaching clients is the importance of niching yourself and how to stand for something different and unique, so you can stand out from your competition.

So what is a Dream Business?

I'm sure your definition might be different than mine, but when I refer to creating a Dream Business when working with my coaching members, this is the definition I use:

A Dream Business:

- Continues to grow even during a crappy economy

- Has multiple streams of revenue

- Becomes an asset for worry-free retirement

- Is always firing on all cylinders

- Is fun to operate

- Provides the lifestyle you want

- Allows you to give back and make a difference in the lives of others

- It can help make your dreams come true!

As I sat on my boat resting from my recent event, I reflected on my presentation, **"Success – Mindset and Money,"** and tried to decipher what was *the* most powerful message I shared during that module.

Honestly, I talked about money, debt, the countless challenges entrepreneurs face, and I also thought about what makes the highly successful entrepreneurs just that – highly successful.

And that's when it hit me.

Highly successful entrepreneurs have an uncanny ability to see opportunity, assess a situation, quickly and deliberately consider the pros and cons, and then DECIDE and move on. They make a decision and act –

one way or the other, and they build greater momentum moving their businesses forward.

The ability to DECIDE in large part comes from confidence, and confidence comes from success and being in action.

Before success, confidence happens when you first DECIDE that enough is enough. It's that moment when you say to yourself, perhaps at 3:00 a.m. when you're lying in bed wondering how to make payroll or whether or not to invest even more of your savings or borrow from someone, anyone, "I am going to keep this dream alive just one more week."

There is a point for most entrepreneurs when the success they want seems to be eluding them; they finally look themselves in the mirror and get real about why they're not taking action, why they're not doing what they know they need to do to grow their Dream Business.

My great friend, Melanie Benson Strick, known as America's Small Business Optimizer, says, "Far too many entrepreneurs are the impediment to their own success." This is true, and Melanie, who is my personal mindset coach (more on that later) kicked me in the butt to start doing what I knew I needed to do to achieve higher levels of success and for that I am forever grateful

With Melanie's help, I finally DECIDED that it was my time, and if I stepped up my game and DECIDED that I would be bold enough to make the tough choices that needed to be made, I too could become the success I knew I could be... and wanted to be.

Doing what needs to be done means different things for different people. However, having coached many entrepreneurs, one of the common places where struggling entrepreneurs get hung up revolves around money and the willingness to put their money where their mouth is. But as Coach Melanie says, "Not willing to do some of the things successful people do and expecting that somehow you can achieve high levels of success anyway – is simply not reality."

What am I talking about? I'll get very transparent with you and share some of the things I KNEW needed to be done, yet I held back. In effect, I decided to "think about it" and perhaps do these things later. Of course I now know that this just put me farther into Squishyville where *nothing* happens.

Here are some things that I was not ready to do and some of the areas I was not willing to invest early in my business and they definitely slowed my growth:

- *Speak to groups of people*
- *Write a book*
- *Create videos*
- *Start a podcast*
- *Hire a coach*
- *Join a mastermind*
- *Host my own seminar or live event*

I knew all of these things would help me grow my business, yet I was bound and determined to become a success *without* doing them because, frankly, they scared the hell out of me. Eventually, I had that 3:00 a.m. moment, and I DECIDED that I was no longer willing to be the impediment to my own success. I decided to man up.

I finally DECIDED that slow-to-no growth was no longer an acceptable option for me (a saying I use often and display at my events) and DECIDED to "go all in" and do what needed to be done to grow my Dream Business and finally live the lifestyle I wanted.

Have you had a 3:00 a.m. moment?

Perhaps you've had many 3:00 a.m. moments.

I want to encourage you to DECIDE right now, this very moment, that slow-to-no growth is no longer an acceptable option for you and your business.

Where is Squishyville?

Let me finish telling you about the title of this book and this chapter, which is highly instructive from a marketing perspective. I told you I was going to be transparent!

DECIDE: There is unquestionably something that *triggers* higher levels of success for some entrepreneurs while others simply struggle to even break six figures. It is the ability to DECIDE!

Decide yes or no, but never "maybe." Maybe leads to Squishyville!

When faced with a challenge, situation, opportunity, or anything else that requires a commitment to do one thing or the other, when a decision needs to be made, some entrepreneurs freeze or many more simply postpone the decision to a later date – the ol' back burner!

The reverse is also true. Some immediately step up to the plate and decide: "yes" or "no," but never "maybe."

Being indecisive will slow you down. It's like tying an anchor around your waist, or in terminology that I prefer, it's like trying to get your boat up on plane while dragging your anchor.

The Ultimate Success Trigger: Having the ability to quickly size up a situation and make a decision – to DECIDE – is what I know is the Ultimate Success Trigger. Looking back on the last 13 years as a business owner, my ability to be comfortable making thousands of decisions, sometimes in rapid succession, has unquestionably given me the ability to create my Dream Business and enjoy the success and lifestyle that come with it.

While many decisions were made in my first five years in business, I recall a REALLY big decision I faced in 2006. After starting my first business in October 2001, five years later I had grown it to multiple six figures.

I was doing okay financially; however, I struggled to live the lifestyle I wanted because, candidly, I was tied to my business.

Oh sure, I was the founder and president of my own corporation, but besides the title on my business card, I was simply the sole employee of a company that I happened to own. I did everything. Can you relate? Are you there now?

In 2006, I realized I had options, and as scary as the decision was, I did DECIDE… to start over!

Today I run several successful six-figure businesses – some multiple six-figure businesses, and the advice, wisdom, and information I share in this book will help you create your Dream Business too. This book will help you get more comfortable with the power to DECIDE and avoid Squishyville.

Our journey toward the Ultimate Success Trigger and your Dream Business begins with an explanation – where is Squishyville?

As I said, when faced with the need to make a decision there are essentially three options: "yes," "no," or "I'll think about it," and I contend that "yes" or "no" are your two best choices. The last option paves the way to Squishyville!

Even if time later proves that you made a wrong decision, you can always take corrective action and keep moving forward. Forward progress is the goal.

Indecision leads to paralysis. Indecision leads right to Squishyville. Remember, success is NOT a straight line. It is perhaps the most crooked line you'll find!

However, when you decide *not* to say "yes" or "no" and instead say, "I'll 'think it over," you go directly to Squishyville, and *nothing ever happens in Squishyville*.

Squishyville might be another name for the "back burner," but the end result is the same. It is a place where growth is slowed and opportunities go to die. Even with the best of intentions to revisit some opportunities later, once you decide *not to decide*, life takes over and 99 percent of the once-good opportunities are long gone. You may think that choosing not to decide is a decision. And perhaps it is, but it's a very bad one.

The Doctor Is In!

In addition to my own experience and sharing the decisions I've made, you're going to benefit from the amazing wisdom, knowledge, and expertise I've learned from working with someone I believe to be the best entrepreneurial mindset coach in the business: my good friend and personal mindset coach, Melanie Benson Strick.

Melanie is known as America's Leading Small Business Optimizer for a reason. She has been blessed with a gift to "see" and quickly ascertain what's wrong in the ol' entrepreneurial brain box and fix it. Melanie helps successful entrepreneurs up the level of their games.

I have had the pleasure of interviewing Melanie many times for the members of No Hassle Newsletters and No Hassle Social Media, my Dream Business Mastermind Group, and on my weekly podcast, Stick Like Glue Radio.

Melanie and I share a love for helping other entrepreneurs achieve higher levels of success, and knowing how important this topic is, when I told her about this book, Melanie graciously gave me permission to use any and all material I have gleaned from our years of working together, both from the interviews I've done and from our personal work together – working on me! I will be including Melanie's insights throughout *DECIDE*. Additionally, I have interviewed a number of entrepreneurs, members of my Dream Business Mastermind and Coaching Program, about some of the key topics I cover in this book and am including their thoughts as well. (Note: complete bios for the entrepreneurs featured in DECIDE are included in the back of the book.)

WARNING: Who I Am Not:

I will be talking about some of the financial decisions I made in the early years of my business, and I want you to know that I am not a financial advisor and honestly have very limited expertise in this area of business.

For financial decisions, you might read books by Dave Ramsey or Suze Orman or consult your own CPA. I have read several of their books and enjoy both of their advice and wisdom on financial matters. I also have a very good CPA.

I want to be very clear with you that some of the choices I made are against what some of the experts advise. I share my story and the decisions I made in some personal detail for two reasons:

First, not every situation you face will be a by-the-numbers, clear cut choice. Sometimes you have to rely on your gut and what your heart is telling you to do.

Second, while the decisions I made may not be what's best for you, I urge you to focus more on and learn from the decisions I made and why. In fact, the biggest lesson to be learned is that I did make tough decisions, invested in my future success, and have ultimately prospered as a result.

To be sure, not every decision worked out the way I wanted, but I have become very comfortable with making fast decisions and benefitting from and adapting to the results of these decisions.

What Else You'll Learn from This Book

This book is not simply about how to make decisions. I will share a lot about the types of decisions you will face that could be holding you back.

In a very personal way, I'm also going to "pull back the curtain" on my business and on myself as a person and entrepreneur and talk about some things that are most often not talked about, especially in what might be called a business success book!

Here's a small sample of what lies ahead and why... again I say... this will be the most important book you'll read about business success:

- *The Impostor Syndrome*
- *How to get comfortable with and attract more money*
- *Entrepreneur vs Small Business Owner – which are you and which should you be?*
- *How to handle the ever present entrepreneurial head trash!*
- *How to become immune to criticism*
- *Do you have the right to be successful?*
- *Five habits of highly successful entrepreneurs*
- *Why it's okay that you're different from your friends*
- *How to know when you're really successful*
- *Why fear is preventing your success*
- *The truth about money and debt*
- *How successful people think differently*

As with my other books, I'll end each chapter with a quick summary and a decision point.

Are you still with me?

Are you ready to be uncomfortable?

Are you ready to face some of your own personal demons –
things that are holding you back from realizing all that you are
capable of?

Are you ready to create your Dream Business?

I often share the first chapter of my books as free gifts for
people who visit my various web sites. Some authors will write the
first chapter of their book in a less harsh or straight forward way to
encourage you to either buy their book or keep reading.

I have purposefully gone the other way for a reason.

DECIDE is not a feel good book full of optimistic quotes
from millionaires and billionaires, nor is it a "rah rah"
entrepreneurial cheerleading book to help you get going. Instead,
DECIDE will hit you right between the eyes with the reality of
what it is like to start and grow a successful business. As I often
tell my coaching clients, building a Dream Business is not for the
faint of heart.

Building a Dream Business is a lot of work, and it requires
a level of intensity, commitment, and perseverance that simply put,
most do not possess. That's why the statistics are what they are.
Half of all small businesses started will fail in the first few years
and 80 percent will fail by year five.

Many will cite "running out of money" as the reason they
fail. I believe that is likely true. Yes, they ran out of money, but I
believe most likely ran out of money because they ran out of guts
and courage to make the tough choices necessary to keep going.

If there were an autopsy done on failing businesses, I'm
willing to bet that many failed because the owner never had that
3:00 a.m. "holy crap" moment. And while many likely had
sleepless nights and the desire to be successful, they never got to
the point where they DECIDED to stop being the impediment to
their own success, to cast their egos aside, to "man up" and do
what's needed to become a success.

I wrote this first chapter of *DECIDE* with an "in your face"
tone for a reason. *DECIDE* is about facing reality and doing what

needs to be done to create your Dream Business. If you're ready to "go all in," then turn to Chapter Two and let's get started.

Pulling the Ultimate Success Trigger:

❖ *There are only two options to any decision: yes or no. "Maybe" or "I'll think about it" leaves you mired in indecision that weighs you down and prevents forward progress.*

❖ *A "maybe" decision leads right to Squishyville, and nothing ever happens in Squishyville.*

❖ *If time and evidence later prove you made an incorrect decision (and it will happen), correct course and move forward again.*

❖ *Good opportunities, when placed on the "I'll think about it back burner" rarely come around a second time.*

❖ *You will face countless decisions and several tough choices in your business. Dedicate yourself to learning to quickly analyze situations and DECIDE.*

DECIDE:

Having completed the first chapter, you have come to the first decision to make, along with space for you to list the pros and cons and your commitment to your decision, whether it's "yes" or "no." A decision for yes or no (a "no" provided that you have solid reasons for it and a plan for an alternative) is acceptable. "Maybe" may be your choice. However, remember that maybe is the choice to head directly to Squishyville.

Is slow-to-no growth an acceptable option for you?

Pros:

_____

_____

_____

_____

Cons:

_____

_____

_____

_____

Yes, here is the action I will take:

_____

No, here is what I will do instead:

_____

Chapter Two: Decide to Take Out the Trash

Head trash most likely affects a majority of people, and entrepreneurs are no exception. In fact, I would argue that because of the risky nature of launching a business, entrepreneurs may be more susceptible.

Head trash is the junk that floats around in our heads. I feel compelled to once again share a disclaimer: I am not a doctor and have zero professional training in psychology. The training and opinions I'll share here are based on my own experience and the experience of many other entrepreneurs that I know and/or have coached. End small print!

Here's Coach Melanie's take on head trash:

Head Trash

Do you have a trash can going on in your mind in which you're polluting your energy by having negative thoughts and junk in your head that you're sorting through all the time? If you have not achieved the level of success that you want, if you're doing all the right things and have given yourself enough time to achieve success but haven't gotten there yet, you probably have some trash that's keeping you from performing at a higher level.

You have to determine the ratio of effort spent and success achieved. If you spend 80 percent of your effort to get 20 percent of your results, it's upside down. You probably have some ineffective strategies or junk and trash going on that is preventing you from seeing greater possibilities.

Look at what is going on in your head all day long. This is a real truth moment. You have to ask yourself how much time you spend worrying about what might happen. How much time are you worrying about being able to pay your bills? How much time do you have going on in your head thinking, "Wow, what happens if this all goes away?" How much of it is fear? How much of it is real joy and power and possibility?

If you have more than 40 percent of your time in fear of some kind, worry or anxiety of some kind, then you really do have some stuff going on that needs to get cleaned up. Personally, if I spend more than ten percent of my time in this state, I'm going to go do a tune up. I just don't want to exist there.

When our brains are running in those negative programs, they are, on some level, sending out negative thought patterns that we're going to start acting from. Those negative thought patterns are almost always destructive.

Head trash is real, and left unchecked, it can be a real business crippler... or killer. The remedy is the same as if your kitchen trash can were overflowing with garbage and "smelling up the joint." The solution? Easy, take out the trash!

While taking out the trash may be easy, let's look at what comprises the trash that exists between your ears. It is the enormous collection of feelings, thoughts, beliefs and experiences that you've been accumulating since you were born. Your kitchen trash can left unchecked becomes stinky and unpleasant. Your head trash left unchecked also becomes stinky and unpleasant. Squishyville is full of residents who, for whatever reason, cannot or refuse to take out their head trash.

As an entrepreneur who presumably wants to achieve great success, you must DECIDE to deal with your own head trash. Left unchecked, paralyzing fear will often be the result of letting your head trash fester. In an upcoming chapter (Decide Not to Be an Impostor), we will talk about the fear of "being found out," and to a large degree, that is a result of head trash and a lack of self-confidence.

Sharing My Own Problems with Head Trash

Let me be vulnerable and share some of my once limiting head trash. Remember the list of things I could refuse to do and still be successful? Don't look back for them, here they are again:

- *Speaking to groups of people*
- *Writing a book*
- *Creating videos*
- *Launch a podcast*
- *Hiring a coach*
- *Joining a mastermind*
- *Hosting my own seminar or live event*

Without a doubt, most of these are things that highly successful entrepreneurs do to grow their businesses. For as long as I can remember, I was terrified to speak in public – so much so that when it came to reading aloud in high school, I was prepared to skip class and take an F rather than face my classmates and read to them. You see, head trash can strike at any age!

As my career started advancing, I became a regional manager with a large staff of people reporting to me. In that position, I had occasional meetings to lead and my escaping or maneuvering around this fear was getting harder by the day. I couldn't take an F! I remember feeling that I could either accept this limitation and take whatever career risk I needed to, or I could fix it – take out the trash – and continue to advance.

When I DECIDE to go all in and fix something, I go all in! The following is short list of what I've done to overcome my fear of public speaking... what I've done to take out this head trash:

- Took the Dale Carnegie program...

  ... and I liked and enjoyed so much that I was an assistant instructor for nine years!

- Did positive affirmations every day for two years (and still do them).

- Joined a local group where speaking every month was a requirement... not an option.

- Underwent hypnosis – both professional and self-hypnosis.

I'm probably omitting some other remedies, but you get the idea. The point is, I had a 3:00 a.m. moment and I DECIDED that I would no longer be the impediment to my own success. One 3:00 a.m. moment occurred after I was asked to speak to a group of successful entrepreneurs led by Bill Glazer and my wonderful friend, Lee Milteer. This was a huge opportunity for me, and as soon as I got the invitation, my heart raced and all the public speaking head trash came rushing back. Thankfully, with everything I had done to "take out this trash," I DECIDED to accept the invitation, and it was a big moment in my newly re-branded Dream Business.

DECISION POINT

Take out your head trash before it stinks up your mindset!

Today I'm comfortable speaking anywhere to any group.

In 2009 when inexpensive flip cameras were developed, posting videos was all the rage. Up to that point, we entrepreneurs could hide behind teleseminars, written words, and web sites. But with this new and now inexpensive technology, people you didn't know were going to see "who you really are" and hear your silly voice... and that made me nervous.

In the chapter "Decide to be Authentic," I talk more about my experience with videos, but once again, I was in a place where I had to DECIDE that no longer would I let my insecurities about being liked or accepted, or sounding silly and potentially made fun of get in the way of me creating my Dream Business with this powerful marketing strategy.

I don't recall the exact 3:00 a.m. moment for this, but it was during the time I was still heavily in debt, and in addition to knowing that a successful growing business would quickly erase my debt, my twin girls also wanted to go to college and no doubt get married. KaChing!

I DECIDED it was time to act, so I dove into videos and never stopped. Over the last six years of creating weekly videos – yes, every week without fail (another lesson there about consistency and persistency, but I digress!) – I will tell you that I've not only become very comfortable doing them, they have produced a lot of money for me! You can view my videos at www.NewsletterGuru.TV.

Another early fear was working with a coach. Once again, time has shown that highly successful people work with coaches. My head trash was that in working with a coach, I would feel that even though I had achieved some success, I would not measure up... and once again, the feelings about being an impostor started filling my brain. Thankfully I DECIDED to do what I knew would help me grow faster, and I've been in mastermind groups and working with coaches ever since. And guess what? As with most fears, it's never as bad as you think... and the upside is huge!

Before moving on, let me tackle one more, quite "fresh" piece of head trash that I've gotten rid of – live events. I've known for years that running your own live event is perhaps *the* best way to grow a coaching business – hands down, no question. And for at least three years, I made one excuse after the other about why I was not hosting my own seminars, when seemingly everyone else in my circle of peers was offering live events.

The head trash was simple yet enormous and loud in my head:

- What if nobody attends?

- What if I bomb and owe a ton of money for the hotel, AV team, caterers, etc.?
- What if I'm successful getting people to attend... and then I totally freeze and suck! Yikes!

As I said, head trash can be paralyzing. Thankfully, through some friendly and not so friendly prodding from my peers and coaches, and honestly through a lot of prayer – I DECIDED that 2014 was MY YEAR!

In 2014, I created my Dream Business Academy live events and sold out two of them. As I write this chapter, we're about 90 days from Dream Business Academy in San Diego, and we're down to only 12 available seats, and guess what – I don't suck! I should have taken out "live event" head trash long ago.

Other Entrepreneurial Head Trash

While I've shared quite a bit about my own head trash and what I did to "take it out," the problem is pretty pervasive among entrepreneurs, so I asked about this when interviewing a few Dream Business Mastermind members and want to take a few minutes to share what they had to say to help you really understand that you are not alone in your own struggle with head trash.

Brad Szollose, consultant and best-selling author of *Liquid Leadership*, shared this with me:

"Most of us have a template hammered into us from our family background and what our mothers and fathers led us to believe. For me, I grew up in a small town with a farming community and a working class. There were two beliefs: One, you must work hard for *every single* penny, and two, there was a poverty consciousness with some religious overtones. This was my head trash throughout the years. My father suggested that as an artist, I'd never make a dime.

"This head trash isn't really conscious, but it becomes a gut feeling. You feel stymied or that you can't move forward. When I first started K2 Design, there was one night at 1:00 in the morning when I was in my backyard on Staten Island, looking up with tears in my eyes asking, 'Why me? Why am I struggling and can't make money?' Then a garbage truck went by in the *opposite* direction of the dump with a giant 'Z' spray painted on it. The Z typically represents the end of something, so it made me laugh. It was a real metaphor for all the trash in my head being carted away, and I started laughing. Tears of sadness turned to laughter and within a year, my company went public.

"Right after that, I started to really analyze why things were going wrong. One of the profound things that came out of that was that I was trying to prove my father wrong my whole life. Once I let that go and decided what was truly driving me, that's when everything shifted."

Gary George, Founder and CEO of Blazin Multimedia, shared this with me regarding the head trash he overcame:

"My head trash happened when I started my television show. No one wanted to join me, and I had to go at it myself. I felt like I would have more courage if I were working with others. I felt really uneasy that others didn't share my vision, but I shook that off and moved forward, and the show became a huge success. Then everyone came out of the woodwork to help.

"Other head trash I had to shake out was due to my age. I was pretty young when I started, so it was a little intimidating. I had to tell myself that I wasn't a kid and could go ahead and carry myself as an adult and move forward."

Another Dream Business Mastermind member, Kelly Roach, Founder and CEO of Kelly Roach Coaching, really shared some information about dealing with head trash that rocked!

"When I first started my business, I was working full time, the breadwinner, and had a high level of responsibility. I said I wanted success but had head trash around fully committing to really growing my business. I wasn't doing everything I could possibly do to build my own business. We can all play a bit of the victim in our own story. There is no shortage of excuses. One day I woke up and realized that I could not expect my business to give me what I was not willing to give my business. For me, it was picking up the phone, connecting with clients, and making sales calls. I had to focus on fundamentals. I caught myself in the idea

DECISION POINT

Decide that you cannot expect your business to give you what you are not willing to give your business!

about wanting what was at the end of the rainbow without rolling up my sleeves doing the work. As soon as I made that change, my business started to grow."

Finally, Susie Miller, speaker, coach, author, and The Better Relationship Coach shared her own words of wisdom about head trash and how it affects you:

"What we believe and think about takes root. What will other people think about me is a big question we all have. It's a driving force in a lot of our lives. What I tell clients as a coach and counselor is that first of all, most people aren't thinking about you. They're thinking about their own insecurities and head trash. Worrying about what other people think of you is allowing them to dictate your future. You are allowing them into the driver's seat instead of you sitting there.

"I'm a firm believer in affirmations, but not the Polly Anna, pie-in-the-sky statements because our subconscious mind can actually work against that. I believe in framing it as being in the process of becoming that which we want to become. For example, 'I'm in the process of becoming disciplined and consistent to grow my business and move it forward.' Or 'I'm in the process of building my savings account to buy a boat or invest in a vacation.' These types of affirmations don't create an argument with our subconscious brains but challenges it to reach those goals and move beyond.

"We also tend to only visualize the end. I teach people to visualize the process. Visualizing the end isn't enough… you have to visualize yourself doing the thing that will get you to your goal."

Different people will react to different stimuli or being pushed to get outside of their comfort zones. I remember a coaching client a few years ago whose business model required him to make cold calls, at least initially until he built momentum. He was paralyzed in fear to make these calls, even though

DECISION POINT

Those who mind don't matter, and those who matter won't mind.

he knew and agreed that they could and likely would turn his business around. During one of our private coaching calls, I could literally hear the fear and depression in his voice. He asked me what I would do. I then asked him for his permission for me to speak candidly and rather bluntly. I told him that he may hate me after this call, or it may be the best call of his life. I was prepared to deliver some tough love, and he said he was prepared to hear it.

This guy had two kids, one in middle school and one in high school. I asked him to consider the message his inaction and fear of doing what he knew needed to be done was sending to his kids. I said, "Suppose your son says he no longer wants to play ball because it's hard and he doesn't want to stink. He'd rather stay home and play video games… what advice would you give him? Would you tell him that it's okay to give up when things are hard? It's okay to retreat to your bedroom to play video games? How does that prepare him for life?"

He was starting to see my point, but I did not back off. I said, "Our kids watch and observe every move we make, and they're going to take their cues about how to live their lives by how you live yours. Your kids may not see you not making the calls, but the end result is the same. You are struggling and they know it. Now let's flip the coin. Suppose you make ten calls a day first thing in the morning. What are the chances that you'll land a client?"

He cited some accurate stats about cold calls and conversions, and I told him that with full pride, he could share his story of DECIDING not to give up just because things were hard, share his story about making cold calls even though they sucked, and then tell his son about the new clients he got as a result. Bottom line, prove to his kids that their dad is not a quitter, and by example, they won't be quitters either.

There was silence on the phone for a while. As uncomfortable as it was, I let it be. He then told me how much he appreciated my tough love, and he committed to making ten calls a day – to start. He did it, and his business grew so much that he was offered a partnership in a large company in his field. I have no doubt that his kids and wife are proud of him and the example he set stepping outside of his comfort zone and doing what was hard because it was necessary. It was not only great for his business and career – it will serve his kids well for many years. He DECIDED to take out his head trash.

You've probably seen several acronyms for fear and most, if not all, are true. Everyone has fears but what separates most entrepreneurs from highly successful entrepreneurs is their ability to DECIDE to push through and step out into a space and place that may be uncomfortable... But guess what – all BIG growth happens outside your comfort zone. Head trash leads to Squishyville, and nothing happens there.

Pulling the Ultimate Success Trigger:

❖ *Everyone has head trash. It's made up of negative, self-limiting thoughts. If you don't take it out, it paralyzes you.*

❖ *Head trash leads to fear: fear to do what you need to do to create your Dream Business and live your dream lifestyle.*

❖ *Consider these FEAR acronyms:*
  o *False Expectations Appearing Real*
  o *Forget Everything and Run*
  o *Finding Excuses and Reasons*
  o *Failure Expected and Received*

❖ *Fear is part of the human existence. Learn to get rid of it when it pops up. You may need to take some big steps and make some tough choices to do so. Just do it... or accept slow-to-no growth.*

DECIDE:

I fully understand head trash and fear and shared my story about DECIDING to overcome my fears. I even had some trepidation about sharing my personal experiences so transparently. I did so to show you that you can get rid of your own head trash and overcome fear.

Should I take out my head trash?

Pros:

_____

_____

_____

_____

Cons:

_____

_____

_____

_____

Yes, here is the action I will take:

_____

No, here is what I will do instead:

_____

Chapter Three:
Decide Not to Be an
Impostor

Every big business starts small.

Many highly successful entrepreneurs running Dream Businesses today started out in a spare bedroom, in a basement office, or at the dining room table. Some refer to this as "bootstrapping," and it is great way to get started building a business without spending a lot of money.

So what's the problem?

For some entrepreneurs, especially those who have come from a corporate background – with all of the benefits and perks of a "real" office and support system – bootstrapping in a spare bedroom or similar locale can lead to something called Impostor Syndrome.

The Impostor Syndrome is sometimes also referred to as the Fraud Syndrome and is a psychological phenomenon in which people are unable to internalize, accept, and feel good about their accomplishments. No matter what you call it, it leads you to Squishyville… the awful place where nothing happens.

This term was first used in an article by Pauline R. Clance and Suzanne A. Imes, and while it can be a real phenomenon where people struggle with success, despite external evidence of their competence and the outward signs that they have achieved a certain level of success, Impostor Syndrome is optional. In essence, you DECIDE to be an impostor.

Now while this is an interesting and debilitating struggle for some, I'd like to spend a few minutes and talk about a much less serious version of Impostor Syndrome that I believe many home-based entrepreneurs struggle with as they market and grow their new businesses. Thankfully, today home-based businesses are much more prevalent and accepted; that was not always the case.

Disclaimer: I am not a doctor and have zero medical or psychological training, so what I'm about to share is based on my own experience and that of many entrepreneurs that I know and have coached. Geez, a lot of disclaimers in this book!

When I first started my business, I set up shop in my dining room. When I started getting some client meetings, I, of course, attended with my fancy-looking business cards and a brochure. We would always meet either in their office or perhaps a restaurant. But other than that, I did what many new entrepreneurs did: I talked a good game about my experience and what I could offer... all the while hoping they wouldn't somehow ask me how I liked working in my dining room, or even how long I'd been in business!

To be clear, that never happened, not even once. But the thought of being "found out" or feeling like someone will label you a fraud weighs heavily on the mind of many entrepreneurs.

I learned later in my career that this is not unusual. So if you sometimes feel like a fraud, you are not alone. I saw a statistic that 70 percent of all people feel like impostors at one time or another, and entrepreneurs are one of the largest groups to wrestle with feelings of worth, achievement, and self-esteem.

Here are some signs that you struggle with Impostor Syndrome:

- Do you ever feel that you don't deserve your success?
- Do you worry that people will find out you are secretly not who you say you are?
- If you achieve some success, do you dismiss it as luck or good timing?
- Do you feel like you've tricked others into thinking you are more successful than you actually are?

What I discovered, and what I hope you will take as good news, is that just recognizing you are feeling certain thoughts and that you are not alone can be a big help and a step in the right direction.

Let's tackle a few of these thoughts and how to reframe them.

Do you ever feel that you don't deserve your success?

You deserve all of the success you can create for yourself. Period. Amen. If you solve problems and provide value to your customers and they reward you for doing so, then congratulations… that is the very essence of business.

In my early days, I used to ask myself, "How hard is it to write a newsletter? And because I've been doing it so long and it's easy for me, how is it fair for me to charge what I want to charge? Especially since I am simply operating out of my dining room!"

BAM – impostor! Or so I thought.

The bottom line is this (and please read or re-read the chapter on Decide

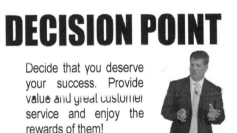

DECISION POINT

Decide that you deserve your success. Provide value and great customer service and enjoy the rewards of them!

to be Profitable): You provide incredible value, backed up with great service, and your customers, clients, or patients appreciate how you make their lives better, so by all means you deserve to be handsomely rewarded. Whether you have a $5,000 per month office or work at your dining table is completely irrelevant.

Do you worry that people will find out you are secretly not who you say you are?

This is really an issue of self-esteem and self-confidence. But it can sometimes also be an issue of exaggeration and over blown marketing! You should always operate your business in the same way you conduct your life: with honor and full integrity.

I never once lied about my home office. If someone asked where my business was located, I had two ready-made answers. I would first say, "I'm located in Eagle, PA." If they asked for more, such as, "Are you in the Eagle View Corporate Center?" I would say, "No, about a mile away." That ended it 99 percent of the time. But occasionally someone would press, and my next answer was that I had home office. And guess what? 99 percent of the time my prospective client would say, "You're so lucky! I wish I didn't have to commute!" The bottom line is to always be truthful; do not make wild claims you can't back up.

If you achieve some success, do you dismiss it as luck or good timing?

This could again be a sign that a more serious conversation is needed, but my view is that everything happens for a reason. There is no luck involved when building a successful business. There are great ideas, good value, massive action, and good marketing. Again, you deserve all the success you work hard to achieve.

Admittedly, there might be times when you decide on a course of action that may be helped along by the timing of external events. For example, you decide to purchase a stock a day before a major announcement causes it to soar. While you could charge that circumstance up to luck or good timing, the truth of the matter is that you DECIDED to buy the stock in the first place.

In the long run, your successful Dream Business will result from your ideas and the value you provide rather than from luck or good timing. Impostor Syndrome results from attributing every single success you have to luck.

Do you feel like you've tricked others into thinking you are more successful than you actually are?

Candidly, when I started out, I struggled with confidence and self-esteem. Some of it was due to my prolonged unemployment and then my bout with cancer. I felt like I was put through the meat grinder for 15 months... and then I started a business. So my initial goals were not big. This is also the reason, as I indicated earlier, I did not want to be a speaker, author, or do many other things that "successful" people do. Part of me thought that I would be tricking others about the level of success I had if I did those things.

However, I DECIDED to do many things to get over my lack of confidence including positive affirmations, self-hypnosis, and mind movies. I learned a lot about these strategies and techniques in *Think and Grow Rich* and *The New Psycho-Cybernetics*, and I also read and listened to countless other success-oriented books from names you no doubt have heard of.

Applying the lessons and strategies of the books I just mentioned took time and effort. It was not simply a matter of *reading* success books. It was a matter of understanding the principles, adopting the strategies, and doing the exercises suggested. There was no trickery involved and results are not instantaneous.

Success becomes a bit like a physical attribute. You're either six feet tall or you're not. You're either successful or you're not. If you are honest and authentic, you don't need to worry about tricking people about your success. It will be as naturally obvious as any physical attribute you may have. Keep in mind this key point: You define your own success! As mentioned earlier, I am not suggesting you ever exaggerate who you are or what you have achieved. Define your success and then work to achieve it.

Achieving Success

Achieving success, however you may define it, quickly eliminates Impostor Syndrome, if you suffer from that affliction. Regardless, Coach Melanie has great information to share regarding achieving success:

Four Pillars of Success

I have a copyrighted model that I use for the Four Pillars of Success. They include knowledge, environment, mindset and habits. I use this to help people understand where they can take control of the things they do that are unconsciously sabotaging their results.

First, do you have the knowledge to be successful? For example, do you have the knowledge of time management along with strategies and techniques to get out of "overwhelm"? What other knowledge, skills, training and education do you need to run your business or move it to the next level?

Next is environment: Do you have the systems, structures, and resources to be successful? For example, do you need to start building a team or, if you have one, is it the right team for the job? What technology could you use or what other support mechanism (like a coach or community) do you need to allow you to raise your way of doing things and get things done more efficiently.

Third, are your habits. A lot of people have really bad habits regarding time management and other areas of business operations. You need to look at the type of actions you take. You may be perpetuating the problem of overwhelm with misaligned habits. Are you someone who plans or fails to plan? Delegate or try to do it all yourself? Do you have the habit of over-committing or under-committing?

Finally, there is mindset. You either have a good belief system that is supporting your growth, or you have a limiting belief system that causes you to see the world through a lens and filter that will never allow you to see what is possible. You might have the attitude that "nobody can do it was good as I can, so why would I ever have anybody else help me?" As a business owner, that thinking is going to get you nowhere!

All four pillars play a part in your ability to love your business and make it grow exponentially.

The bottom line: What helped me the most was finally DECIDING that enough was enough and that I was going to do everything I could to turn the "confidence" corner. The funny thing about confidence is that is becomes easier to achieve and easier to deal with (from an impostor position) when you are in massive action and making things happen in your business. At some point, I realized that it no longer mattered where my "corporate office" was. What was much more important was the value I was providing and being rewarded for.

Pulling the Ultimate Success Trigger:

❖ *Countless successful businesses began with bootstrapping; however, bootstrapping can also lead to Impostor Syndrome – the inability to feel good about what you've accomplished.*

❖ *If you are struggling to accept deserving your success, despite outward signs and external evidence that you are successful, you are suffering from Impostor Syndrome.*

❖ *Do you have any of the Impostor Syndrome symptoms?*

  o *Do you ever feel that you don't deserve your success?*

  o *Do you worry that people will find out you are secretly not who you say you are?*

  o *If you achieve some success, do you dismiss it as luck or good timing?*

  o *Do you feel like you've tricked others into thinking you are more successful than you actually are?*

❖ *You are the only person who can define what it means for you to be successful.*

❖ *The Four Pillars of Success include knowledge, environment, mindset, and habits.*

DECIDE:

Impostor Syndrome affects many small business owners and entrepreneurs who are in the early stages of creating their Dream Businesses. Remember, Impostor Syndrome is a matter of your mindset. Impostor Syndrome is optional!

Do you want to overcome Impostor Syndrome?

Pros:

_____
_____
_____
_____

Cons:

_____
_____
_____
_____

Yes, here is the action I will take:

_____

No, here is what I will do instead:

_____

Chapter Four:
Decide to Be Authentic

The power and freedom of simply being you.

It is not uncommon for entrepreneurs to struggle with their "personal" brand versus their "professional" brand. Or perhaps better stated: Who they are "on the job" versus who they are "off the clock" – so to speak.

This challenge has never been more apparent or even problematic than it is now due to the incredible rise of social media. There is no hiding anymore.

The truth is you can no longer have your "entrepreneurial" brand and a clear and separate "personal" brand that you wish or feel should be off limits and not used when a client or prospective client is considering working with you.

It may feel unfair or somehow too judgmental when a prospective client uses what you consider to be the "personal side" when considering hiring you, but consider the following example.

Suppose you are a parent looking for a nanny and after the interviews, you really like both the applicants' credentials and resumes. Then, after they leave, you do a quick search on Facebook or other Internet search and see pictures of what you consider to be less than safe or appropriate behavior.

I'm not being judgmental of what someone does in their private life, but the fact remains: for many parents seeing such pictures would be unsettling to say the least and a disqualifier for most.

Truthfully, as entrepreneurs, giving this even more than one second's thought or deliberation about how this might be unfair is a complete waste of time and energy. If you get caught up in worrying about what you deem unfair about this, you are bound for Squishyville. For better or worse, this is the world we live in. There is no hiding who you are.

Let me give one more "parent-themed" example. My wife and I have raised four kids (thankfully she did 90 percent of the work!), and as they are now all mature adults living on their own, we have seen many examples of our "leading by example" in the way our kids live their lives.

Just like your kids are watching how you live your life and are learning from and making decisions from the examples you set, your customers and prospects are also drawing conclusions from the way you live your life and, more importantly, what they see of how you live your life.

DECISION POINT

Authenticity is far easier than trying to keep track of the lies you may tell about your skills or your business.

So the question is: As an entrepreneur who wants to achieve higher levels of success, how do you use the fact that we are all operating in an online and ever-connected world... and use it to grow your business?

The answer is simple and actually quite relieving!

DECIDE to be your authentic self – all the time. There should not be a personal brand and a separate "small business owner" brand.

So what do I mean by being authentic? The dictionary describes authentic as "not false or an imitation, true to one's own personality, spirit, or character." The key is authenticity all the time and in every place.

The relieving part for many is that when you choose to drop the corporate facade and be authentic, you can simply be the genuine un-edited version of yourself. This reminds me of the expression "the truth shall set you free!" When you are always authentic and truthful, you don't have to remember what you told to whom and when!

Practically speaking, how does this work as you build your business?

I learned the powerful lesson of being authentic when I started doing my weekly videos in 2009. At first I tried to be the consummate professional businessperson; I kept a business-like straight face and delivered in an authoritative tone some smart business advice.

The trouble was – while I do have some good business advice and wisdom to share, I'll be the first to admit that I am not a "buttoned up" professional businessman! The result did not come across at all how I intended. It was not authentic.

The real authentic me occasionally messes up my words, and more than often my brain and mouth are in a race to see what comes out first. I also like to laugh, wear casual clothes, and talk about my grandson and pets. And while I don't flaunt it, I'm not shy about being a Christian. I love to serve and help others, and I get genuinely excited when I help other entrepreneurs with an idea or tip that helps them get their business going and growing. When this happens, I honestly feel like a kid in a candy store, and when I retell such a story on camera, it shows!

If you watch my videos today, you will see that I am not only unscripted, but I am 100 percent comfortable being who I am – I am the authentic self I just described.

I'm reminded of a time when I was speaking to a couple hundred entrepreneurs about entrepreneurial success and on this trip my wife, Stephanie, went with me, so we could stay a few extra days for some R&R. After my presentation about being my authentic self, someone approached Stephanie in the back of the room and asked, "What's Jim like at home?" She replied, "You just saw it, he's like that all the time!"

If you think the importance of authenticity doesn't matter, consider the story of Brian Williams, the anchor of *NBC Nightly*

News. While covering the war in Iraq in 2003, he was embedded with troops that included flying with a convoy of helicopters in a combat zone. The convoy took on enemy fire. In recalling the events 12 years later, Williams said his helicopter was shot down. The truth? It was another helicopter in the convoy that was shot down, not the one in which Williams as a passenger.

The result? He was suspended without pay for six months, and as I write this, investigations are ongoing regarding other claims he made regarding what he personally witnessed while covering the news and reporting the stories.

The real fall-out? He may have forever jeopardized the career that he worked for decades to build and one that eventually positioned him at the top of his field. The viewing public may forget about his lying, or at the very least wildly exaggerating the account of what really happened, by the time he returns in six months (if he does), but there will always be a question about his authenticity.

Without a doubt, honesty is always the best policy!

The Good and Bad About Being Authentic

If you agree with me, and decide to flip the switch and drop your double persona – and simply be your authentic self all the time, you will attract a lot more of the people you are meant to attract, but you will also repel more of the people you are not ideally suited to work with.

If this troubles you, my advice is to get over it. You're not meant to please or work with everyone, and life is too short to even try to play that game.

So what about social media and authenticity?

A quick last word about being authentic in a social-media-driven world:

From a marketing perspective, as an entrepreneur or small business owner, I believe it is your job to be authentic. However, this does not give you freedom to share your every view on every hot topic.

How then is this being authentic, you might ask, if I'm suggesting that you keep your mouth shut at times?

That's a fair question. Let me tell you first that the only reason I choose to be on any social media platform is to build my brand and grow my business, that's it!

I use social media to stay connected with current customers and clients and showcase who I am and what I have to offer – such as my coaching programs, No Hassle Newsletters, No Hassle Social Media, etc. To that end, I will authentically share things about me that help create and support that brand and image. Social media helps prospects get to know who I am.

What I do not post and share are my feelings on certain hot topics or the flash point of the day. I guess the best way to know what this means is the old adage that cab drivers use: do not discuss sex, politics or religion!

Just like you, I have my own opinions about local and world affairs. But as a growth-oriented entrepreneur, I believe two things:

1. Sharing my views on topics not relevant to my business will not move the ball forward as it relates to building my business.

2. Except for a few close friends, who the heck cares what Jim Palmer thinks anyway?!?

Just because social media exists doesn't mean you have to bare your soul and share your feelings, and the cold hard truth is who really cares anyway!

I'm sure you've seen some threads on Facebook where someone says something provocative, and the next thing you know there are 45 comments from people each arguing their position. It's not a case of who is right and who is wrong. In my opinion, such a thread leaves people feeling uneasy – potential customers.

If you want to use social media to debate, share your opinions and views on different topics, then that is your option.

However, if you are an entrepreneur who wants to use social media as another platform to spread your message, the bottom line is this: Stay focused on who you are, what you offer, what your brand is, and continuously generate content to support that brand, and who you are – and do it in an authentic way.

Along those lines, Coach Melanie has developed a formula to aid in making decisions that's also applicable to your decisions about using social media:

Green Light Formula

One of the checks and balances that can help you ensure you're optimizing every investment, decision, and new opportunity is to ask yourself a few key questions. I call it the Green Light Formula.

First ask, "If I say yes to this, how is it going to get me to my ultimate goal? Is it aligned or is it a distraction?" I believe a lot of people say yes to things that have absolutely nothing to do with making the business they have more successful. They get distracted.

The next question is: "How will this make me money?" We're in business to make money not have a hobby. Taking on a task because it's fun or because you know how to do it leads to spending too much of your time on something that's not profitable.

Finally, ask, "What will I be saying 'no' to if I say 'yes' to this?" We think we're super-heroes and can do it all, but we can't. We don't really have that much bandwidth, and we don't really have that much time. You have to be aware of what is going to be sacrificed along the way.

There has to be a level of accountability, so you're not chasing things anymore wondering if they're going to work. Instead get facts that will help you discern and build that muscle of making good decisions, so you are optimizing.

Trying to have two personas – business and personal – is far more effort than it's worth and ultimately becomes a road block as you build your business. You are who you are, so be authentic.

Pulling the Ultimate Success Trigger:

❖ *With the pervasiveness of social media, it is impossible to have an entrepreneurial brand and personal brand separate from it.*

❖ *There's no hiding who you are. Nor should you want to. By being authentic, you'll attract those people with whom you are best suited to work, and while you will also repel some people, those are the people who would be a poor fit for your business and success.*

❖ *Spend your time and efforts with social media advancing your business rather than sharing your thoughts on the hot topic of the day.*

❖ *Use the Green Light Formula of asking and answering three questions for every decision you make.*

DECIDE:

Be authentic. Although you may think it is unfair for your prospects and clients to judge you, they will. They want to do business with someone they know, like, and trust. Conversely, it makes sense for you to do business with people you like as well.

Should I drop the double persona I may have created?

Pros:

_____
_____
_____
_____

Cons:

_____
_____
_____
_____

Yes, here is the action I will take:

_____

No, here is what I will do instead:

_____

Chapter Five:
Decide to Invest

Highly successful entrepreneurs understand the value and importance of investing in their future growth and profitability.

I believe in every situation there is the "current" you (and your business) and there is the "future" you and business you want – your Dream Business. The fastest way to go from your current situation to your Dream Business is to buy speed. That's right – you can buy speed, or the proper terminology would be you can "invest" in speed.

If you want to get somewhere faster, ask someone who has made the journey before you for the best route! I'm not at all a fan of reinventing the wheel, and my ego is such that I don't care who gets the credit for the idea or roadmap as long as I get where I want to go faster.

There are many places in your business where investing comes into play, but no area is more important than in coaching or masterminding.

Whenever I'm speaking to entrepreneurs and mention masterminding, I get sometimes get questions about accountability groups and how they differ or are similar to a mastermind group.

To be blunt, most accountability groups are "feel good" sessions. I understand the need for them. Bill Glazer, the past president of Glazer Kennedy Insider's Circle and one helluva a marketer, once said that being an entrepreneur is the loneliest job on the planet. Bill is correct; it is lonely, and that's one of the reasons that entrepreneurs like to be part of various groups.

But there is a major difference between being in an accountability group and being in a paid mastermind group.

One of the big differences between *investing* in a coach or mastermind group versus your no-cost accountability groups or non-paid mastermind groups is that paid mastermind groups are run or led by an experienced coach. Successful entrepreneurs/coaches will (or they should!) "get in your face" and occasionally deliver what I call "tough love."

By and large, accountability groups are feel good sessions whereas investing in the right business coach will accelerate your growth. You'll feel tough love, but you will ultimately feel good about your success. Invest with the right coach or mastermind and you are purchasing speed.

So much of success depends on having the right mindset about money, investing, and having courage. Since I just mentioned coaching and masterminding, let me relate a story that will help make this clearer.

In the last few weeks, I've had a couple people speak to me about joining my Dream Business Mastermind and Coaching Program. The conversations were eerily similar.

Both mentioned that they've been following me for a couple years, watch my videos, listen to my podcasts, and read my books, etc. They believed that I was the business coach who could help them finally get to six figures and create their Dream Businesses. After hearing that, the conversations then went something like this:

Me: Great, I appreciate your kind words, I'm ready to get started and help you – what's holding you back?

Prospect: Well, I'm already in a mastermind group.

Me: Tell me about the group you're now in – how long have you been in it?

Prospect: I've been in it three years and I really love the people in the group, many of us have become friends. Although candidly, I'm just not getting what I need from the group to help me grow my business.

Me: I understand the importance of friends, but if the group is not meeting your needs, may I ask why you are still in such a group?

Prospect: Honestly Jim, it's less expensive than your group, and as I said, I'm friends with most of the people in the group and I'd feel bad if I left.

This is a conversation that happens more than a couple times each month, and to be honest, while my heart breaks for people like this because I know they'll likely remain stuck for months if not years and not reach their goal of creating a Dream Business, my intuition tells me that they are not... and likely will never be ready for or comfortable with fast growth... the type of growth that's possible when you invest in speed and experience. These folks have effectively "set up shop" in Squishyville.

People like this are stuck in their own bad habits, and here is Coach Melanie's take on that:

Sabotaging Habits

We all have certain strategies that we're running that are designed specifically to keep us stuck right where we are. To me, that's one of the most important reasons why we have to look at our mindset because once you become aware of the sabotaging habits you might have or the behaviors associated with getting less than desirable results, you can make a decision to get optimum performance in your business now. And optimum performance really means that you learn how to switch gears from doing just enough or from being in reactionary mode to being in proactive power mode.

For example, let's say you're going to host a workshop in March. You're excited. You think, "Yeah, that will be great because at the workshop I'll sell some of my programs. I'll sell some of my products. We'll have a big burst of income." You have that plan for the future, but you don't actually write down all the steps and reverse engineer what you need to do to have a successful number of people in that room who are designed to buy from you. So now you get caught up in doing some things to make money right now. You get distracted by some other projects. You have a lot of stuff on your plate. And the time's creeping by.

You get through January and you think, "Oh yeah, I've got that event coming up. I can't wait to get to that." But there are more distractions in the moment, reactionary projects, clients needing stuff, and your timeline slips. The next thing you know it's a month before your event and you're like, "Oh my gosh, I haven't even started marketing it yet. I'll just push myself really hard. I can do it."

What's happening inside that strategy is you're becoming a sprinter. You get yourself under so much pressure because you wait to really get into action around big ideas and big projects and big payday opportunities. You put them off because you're not really that organized with your time and your schedule. And the next thing you know, you're pushing yourself. You're driving yourself. You're overwhelmed. You're exhausted. You set unrealistic expectations. And you are leaving tons of money on the table because you didn't take enough time to properly market and plan out the success of that event.

That's a type of strategy that I see in 70 percent of the entrepreneurs I mentor and coach. They know what to do. They're smart. They're capable. But they haven't necessarily learned how to properly set up and manage themselves and the projects and the opportunities that they put in their schedules. So they're constantly pushing themselves at the last minute to pull things off without enough time and enough bandwidth to get things done right.

Conversely, in power mode and in proactive mode, you decide, "Here's what I'm going to make this year successful. Here's how I'm going to do it." You put a plan together for about a year in which you reverse engineer who you have to be and what you have to do to achieve that income goal.

So instead of asking every 30 days, "What am I going to do to make money now?" you're working a plan and you have a machine in motion that automatically starts to generate success. One of the biggest things I think is missing in our culture and in our entrepreneurial communities is that we have learned the strategy of being reactionary, instead of being proactive and really making a commitment to slow down, so you can multiply and exponentially grow the results you have.

Are You Prohibiting Your Own Growth?

Let me ask you to have a "get real" moment with yourself right now and use the situation I described about the small business owner not wanting to join my mastermind group as the barometer of how much you truly want to achieve higher levels of success. Have you been or are you now spending your hard-earned dollars or, worse yet, spending your precious limited time being part of a group or other situation that is not helping you grow?!?

Further, is the reason you are still there because you don't want to offend someone? If so, as your coach (at least while you're reading this book), I'd like to deliver some tough love:

Stop it now or forever be happy with the business and lifestyle you currently have.

If you meet, talk to, and interact with enough highly successful entrepreneurs, you'll learn one thing. They are not afraid to make the tough decisions necessary to move their businesses forward, and they are not concerned with hurting people's feelings.

None of them are rude or intend to hurt feelings; instead what they are is driven. They are driven to success with a level of desire and intensity that few people have. That's why the top one to two percent exists. It's because we are all wired differently, and you have to decide if you truly have what it takes to DECIDE that slow-to-no growth is no longer an acceptable option.

You have to DECIDE that you will no longer play in the shallow end of the pool when all the growth is happening in the deep end.

You have to DECIDE whether or not you are truly committed to do whatever it takes to make your dream become reality.

It's time for you to DECIDE.

I want to contrast the story above with that of a new entrepreneur who chose a different path and in doing so displayed courage and has benefited and profited as a result.

In the fall of 2012, I started to help someone start a new home-based VA (virtual assistant) business, so she could quit her job and become a stay-at-home mom in the spring. This client essentially did everything I told her to do and within nine months had built a business that was bringing in more revenue than her old salaried position. If you know me or follow me closely, you might recognize that story as that of my daughter, Jessica Rhodes. Jessica founded Entrepreneur Support Services, so she could be a stay-at-home mom to my grandson, Nathan.

DECISION POINT

Decide to put your money where your mouth is and put skin in the game. It WILL make a difference.

Now while I love my daughter very much, I also believe in teaching valuable lessons, so she received six months of coaching in exchange for working for my business doing client support work. Sorry, no free lunch!

In December 2013, one year later, Jessica said that she wanted to join a mastermind group and having heard so much about mine, she wanted in. I told her that she would make a great addition to our growing group of action-oriented entrepreneurs and that all she had to do was get out her credit card and register!

Candidly, I think this caught Jessica a little off guard. However, when I told her she would take my advice and the experience more seriously if she had to invest, she agreed and joined the program. Two months later, having made two monthly payments, she told me she was not happy with the growth she'd seen so far and declared that she wanted to "step it up" and double her current sales and have a six-figure business before the end of the year.

Her question to me was, "Is it possible and how do I do that?"

My answer: "Of course it's possible, and the easiest way to do it is to do exactly as I tell you and don't question me!"

She agreed, and I'm very proud to say that she hit her goal of having a six-figure business by July!

Lest you think I'm merely bragging about my daughter or puffin' up my chest as a business coach, let me share a few valuable lessons from this story:

1. Jessica put skin in the game from day one – no free rides or sense of entitlement.

2. When she wanted to join the mastermind, although her dad was the coach, she had to play by the same rules as everyone else.

3. Jessica followed my every instruction, which I imagine is not always easy. Forget the coach/client relationship, I'm also her dad!

The reason I asked her if she would do everything I told her to do was easy. I have done this so many times that I knew exactly what Jessica had to do if she wanted to get to six figures fast, starting with her being willing to set aside her blooming entrepreneurial ego and let someone else steer the ship.

Here's the secret: Seeking wisdom, knowledge, and guidance is prudent. The most successful entrepreneurs have an insatiable appetite for knowledge and information.

The real question is whether you want to be successful and prosperous enough to care whose idea it is?!?

Today, Jessica runs two successful enterprises: www.EntrepreneurSupportServices.com and www.InterviewConnections.com.

Here's another example of purchasing speed by investing in your future growth and profitability:

In 2006, I was starting my new business model, and by plan, I was losing some clients from my first business through attrition. My plan was to slowly close Dynamic Communication while ramping up No Hassle Newsletters and my other online offerings.

As with many plans, the timing doesn't always work out, and I found myself in a severe cash flow crunch – again!

In early 2007, I had the opportunity to exhibit at a major national marketing event. This event would have about 1,000 entrepreneurs in attendance most of whom already understood the value of a company newsletter. If there were ever a prime event for me to exhibit at, this was it.

The challenge was that between exhibition fees, the cost of travel, and a display, this decision meant an investment of $7,000 to $8,000 to make it happen. With cash flow super tight and me still paying down early debt, this was obviously a huge decision.

I considered the pros and cons of waiting, paying down more debt, and hoping to exhibit at a future event versus "going all in" and ramping up sales faster. It seemed like a roll of the dice either way, but here's what convinced me to "go all it":

1.   You cannot save your way out of debt; you *grow* your way out of debt.

2.   Generally, those businesses first to market are able to carve out their position.

3.   I am an impatient person!

I believed in my heart and gut that what I was offering was awesome and that I simply needed to get in front of enough people.

The bottom line is, despite my financial situation at the time, I rolled the dice on myself and my Dream Business, bit the bullet, and invested in my future... and it paid off. That single event put me in front of 300-plus prospects – many of them became clients over time.

Clearly it doesn't always work out this well, but what I want you to understand most is that investing in yourself is the right thing to do, and yes, when you make smart investments, you can purchase speed and accelerate your growth.

Pulling the Ultimate Success Trigger:

❖ *You can "buy" or "invest" in speed with coaching or by joining a mastermind group. Don't use your time and resources reinventing the wheel.*

❖ *There is a huge difference between a no-cost accountability group and a true mastermind group. Putting skin in the game and making a financial commitment makes a difference and alters your mindset.*

❖ *Seeking wisdom, knowledge and guidance is prudent. The most successful entrepreneurs have an insatiable appetite for knowledge and information.*

DECIDE:

Investing in yourself and effectively "purchasing speed" to accelerate your growth to create your Dream Business faster has proven to be effective for countless entrepreneurs like you. It's time for you to decide whether or not you will do the same.

How can I purchase speed and invest in myself?

Pros:

_____

_____

_____

_____

Cons:

_____

_____

_____

_____

Yes, here is the action I will take:

_____

No, here is what I will do instead:

_____

Chapter Six:
Decide to Delegate... or
Stay Small

One of the most important decisions an entrepreneur needs to make to get to six figures and then to move on and create a multiple-six-figure Dream Business is to release and let go. This chapter could make an amazing difference in your business with just three words – "delegate or die!"

At the very least, it's "delegate or go directly to Squishyville"... do not "Pass Go" and do not collect additional revenue and higher profits.

This mindset challenge is one that trips up far too many entrepreneurs, and it is essential that you climb and conquer this entrepreneurial mountain if you truly want to create a dream lifestyle.

In the beginning, most entrepreneurs start their businesses on day one, armed with an idea, a skill, or talent they want to bring to market and build a business. Whether you're a dentist, lawyer, accountant, or web site developer, you have a talent that solves problems, provides value, and fills a need. That is the essence of a successful business.

But something happens between the time you get your business cards and hang out your shingle and when your growth becomes impeded because you're not willing to release and let go. This chapter will shed some light on potentially what's holding you back, and I hope the story and information I share will help you DECIDE to act... DECIDE to release!

In most cases, I think it's fair to say to every entrepreneur initially wear many hats running a small business. In addition to your "skill" hat (whatever you do), you also wear the hat of other personnel within a typical company such as the accountant, customer service rep, delivery person, janitor, head of marketing, legal advisor, and about a hundred more!

You will be stuck in slow-to-no growth mode and Squishyville if you do not decide to delegate. Do it!

To be clear: recognize that every big business starts small. As sales grow, so do the demands for the time and attention of the entrepreneur and business owner. The stumbling block for many entrepreneurs occurs when they hold on too long to the notion that they can do it all – the lean and mean approach.

One common expression you'll hear around the entrepreneurial water cooler is, "I can do it faster, cheaper, and better than anyone else."

Now if I took some creative license and got into the mindset of many entrepreneurs in a safe environment where full disclosure occurs, the full version of that expression probably sounds like this:

"I can do 'it' faster, cheaper, and better than anyone else, and I'll be darned if I'm going to pay someone to do something I can clearly do myself. I want that all the money in my pocket. I also do not want to hire additional support personnel until I reach a certain point where I can no longer do it all myself."

Do these words ring true for you? Have you actually said them to someone? Or at least thought them on more than one occasion?

Over the course of my entrepreneurial journey, I've gone from being an "I can do it faster, cheaper, and better than anyone else" entrepreneur to having a support team of nine plus people. And every time I hire someone new, my gut twinges slightly, so I ask myself two really important questions:

- Is this new person truly essential to my company and necessary for our continued growth?
- Will this new person either free me up or free up some other key person on my team, so we can implement more and move this business forward at a faster rate of speed?

Here's the bottom line regarding personnel: You should hire slow and fire fast, but if you need to hire to keep growing – then hire! I created a video on this topic for Newsletter Guru TV and in delivering the message I likened it to this expression: If you're thirsty, you should have already been drinking.

If you feel like things aren't getting done and your progress and speed are not what they should be, you should be delegating!

What's even truer is that you do not hire anyone unless they're going to increase your profits. That is really the only reason to "invest" in additional help – to help you make more money! What's important to keep in mind here is that the person you hire is going to help you increase profits by **growing** your business. Don't fall back to the "I'm not going to pay someone to do something I can do myself" mentality, thinking that doing it yourself leaves more money in your pocket. That mentality leads to slow-to-no growth. That mentality leads to Squishyville.

Invest Money to Make Money

The leap that eludes some entrepreneurs is that at certain times it becomes essential to invest money to make more money.

You might be asking, "How is it that I will keep more money when I'm spending more money on payroll?" It's a fair question and as with other parts of this book, I'll share some of my story with you.

In 2006 just as I was once again starting over, rebranding myself, and getting started in Internet marketing and the information marketing business, I decided that I needed a new web site (or two), and I also needed to learn about merchant accounts, auto responders, and a bunch of other things that were new to me.

At this point, I had five years under my belt as an entrepreneur, and for the most part I did everything – the ol' chief cook and bottle washer! However, I had grown a multiple-six-figure business by myself, so I wondered, "Where's the harm?!?"

The harm was that my time was completely maxed out, and to be candid, so was my skill level in some new and important areas – areas critical to my ability to grow and become more profitable. Now, I may not be the sharpest knife in the drawer, so one option was to study and learn what I needed to learn and get it done myself.

Thankfully, I was in my first mastermind group at the time, and when I talked about all that I was doing already as a solo act and what more I wanted to do, I was almost laughed at. At least it felt like it!

One of the more successful entrepreneurs told me that I needed to get a VA (virtual assistant). "What's a virtual assistant?" I asked... and the answer changed my life!

A virtual assistant is someone who works for you on a project-by-project basis. They are a 1099 contract worker – usually they are also entrepreneurs, and they do certain tasks to help other entrepreneurs grow.

I hired my first VA later that month, and that person is still with me today, along with at least eight others. Was it scary to take on the expense of additional help? Absolutely! But it didn't take me long to realize that with the new "extra" time I had created by me not doing tons of task-oriented stuff, I was able to get more important work done. I was able to do the type of work that was allowing me to grow!

This new movement in my business has snowballed to where I have a team of nine VAs who perform a number of tasks to help me run my various businesses. What I focus the majority of my time on these days is working with my coaching clients and marketing my business!

Both of these categories are what I refer to as "high revenue generating" activities.

Here's the deal: If you want to earn a million dollars per year, you need to be doing work that is worth $400 an hour (figuring 50 hours per week and 50 weeks per year). And every minute that you are doing task-oriented stuff, that you could pay someone to do for you for $10 to $60 an hour, then you are holding yourself back. Would you rather earn $400 an hour or $10 to $60 an hour?

The Pareto principle comes into play here. Named for economist Vilfredo Parcto, this concept examines the unequal relationship between input and output, and for many phenomena, 20 percent of the input often creates 80 percent of the output. For the entrepreneur, 20 percent of the effort generates 80 percent of the revenue or 20 percent of the clients generate 80 percent of the sales. Think about your own efforts and results, and you will very likely see the Pareto principle at work.

The opposite can also happen: 80 percent of your efforts generate only 20 percent of the results. If you are concentrating on task-oriented activities… the ones you should be delegating… you have it backward, and I can assure you that you are on the road to Squishyville.

Coach Melanie refers to this as a "derailer," and there are other derailers to be mindful of as you operate your business.

Derailers

There are things that derail your efforts to be successful… "derailers." The first one is a boundary issue, specifically boundaries on your time. If you have not set a time to stop working, your activities will expand to the level you'll work. You may waste time putting out fires for other people on your team, and that prohibits you from focusing on getting the right things done – the things that have the biggest impact.

Remember the Pareto principle: You should be putting 20 percent of your time into things that get you 80 percent of your results. I've had a lot of clients who get this upside down and then burn out quickly.

Look at what you put first in your day. Is it email or handling incoming questions that can wait or is it a project that is going to provide results? I will acknowledge that sometimes it's scary to set boundaries in place, tell people "no," or renegotiate deals that are really destructive for you, but without boundaries you will be derailed.

Another derailer is disorganization. I would estimate that the large majority of business owners that I work with are so disorganized! They don't check their emails for a week or two, lose materials that I send, don't put things on their calendars properly. As a business owner, your job is to get the information you need to do well. Get organized.

You need systems, structure, processes, and a way to manage the flow in your life. Without that, people will see you as disorganized and lose trust in their ability to work with you. Disorganization erodes your confidence and energy, leading you to believe that you don't have time when the real problem is you not putting the right things first.

Being organized pays dividends. Take five minutes to organize and get five hours back. If you take a half hour to get yourself organized, you can almost get a week's worth of time and energy back.

If you are trying to "do it all because you don't want to pay someone else to do something you can do," **you** are the bottleneck to growing your Dream Business.

Dr. Anthony Weinert, physician and surgeon of the foot and ankle, Founder and CEO of Stop Feet Pain Fast Institute, shared his experience with delegating and investing in his own future: "You need to use other people who can help do the things that are non-revenue producing. That freed my time to focus on the areas where perfection really mattered from me. Make a list of things you feel can be handed off to someone else. Don't micromanage feeling you have to do it all yourself.

"I wouldn't put much money toward advertising or coaching because I thought I was wasting it. Looking back, I only wished I had done it earlier. Investing in my practice is what grew my practice. You have to take the leap and have confidence about the result. Put a dollar bill into a machine and have $100 come out. That's how I look at things now."

As I said in the beginning of this chapter, delegate or die. Delegate or learn to get comfortable in Squishyville, learn to accept slow-to-no growth and understand that you will not be able to build your Dream Business and live the lifestyle you want.

Pulling the Ultimate Success Trigger:

- ❖ *It's simple: delegate or die, or at the very least suffer slow-to-no growth in your business.*
- ❖ *While you probably started your business wearing many hats, if you want to grow your business, you absolutely must free up more of your time to focus on the business rather than on necessary but non-revenue producing busy work.*
- ❖ *Just because you might have the skills to accomplish the task-oriented stuff (like keeping your own books or*

doing your own taxes), it doesn't mean you should!
Most "tasks" are necessary but don't spur growth.

❖ *Ask these two questions when considering a hire:*

  ○ *Is this new person truly essential to my company and necessary for our continued growth?*

  ○ *Will this new person either free me up or free up some other key person on my team, so we can implement more and move this business forward at a faster rate of speed?*

❖ *You have to invest money to make money.*

❖ *Apply the Pareto principle: concentrate 20 percent of your time and effort on the things that will generate 80 percent of your results.*

❖ *Be aware of "derailers": failure to set boundaries, working the Pareto principle in reverse, and disorganization.*

DECIDE:

Learning to delegate is one of the single most important lessons to grow your business to six figures and create your Dream Business. Without delegation, you'll suffer slow-to-no growth and end up in Squishyville.

Do you want to delegate?

Pros:

_____

_____

_____

_____

Cons:

_____

_____

_____

_____

Yes, here is the action I will take:

_____

No, here is what I will do instead:

_____

Decide to Delegate... or Stay Small

Chapter Seven:
Decide to Be Immune to Criticism

Criticism. It's everywhere. No doubt you have already gotten your fair share of it. Some of it may be warranted, but a lot of it should probably be ignored. That can be difficult to do; however, you must DECIDE to become immune to criticism. DECIDE to grow a thick skin. If you want to be successful and really grow your business and boost your profits, you simply cannot need the approval from others about how you operate your business.

Very simply, the only folks you need to please are your paying customers, and what they have to say is really the only thing you should be listening to in the first place. Most of the other criticism you will hear does nothing for your business. If you choose to listen to it, you have pointed yourself in the direction of Squishyville and are heading that way.

I believe some entrepreneurs let criticism cloud their judgments, and worse, alter the way they do business. They're afraid of what others think of them and are also afraid of failure. The funny thing about failure is that it often parallels success. Too often, success and failure are depicted as opposites. The road sign to success points one way, and the sign to failure points in the opposite direction. In fact, those roads usually overlap for a time. There is story after story about famous people who reached success by failing. When they hit a road block, instead of traveling in the opposite direction, they stuck to the road they believed would lead to success until they reached the fork – the place where success and failure finally diverged. That's when they reached success.

Think about these examples: Henry Ford went broke five times before he succeeded; Albert Einstein's teacher described him as "mentally slow" and the University of Bern rejected his Ph.D. dissertation as "irrelevant and fanciful"; Walt Disney was fired from his newspaper job for lack of ideas and, like Ford, went broke several times before building Disneyland; Louis Pasteur ranked 15 out of 22 in chemistry; Douglas MacArthur was denied admission to West Point twice before being accepted; Babe Ruth, once the record holder for home runs, was also the record holder for strike outs.

I could fill this whole book with examples of famous successes that were finally achieved because the individual refused to give up... and refused to believe that success lay in the opposite direction from which they were traveling. They believed in their ideas, and they stuck to them. They refused to give up, and most importantly, they were immune to criticism. While most folks don't want to fail, and no entrepreneur sets out to fail, it happens. Accept it; learn from it; move on. Don't be afraid of failure, and don't let a fear of what other people will think or say if you do fail stand in your way.

An Incredible Example of Immunity to Criticism

In the fall of 2012, Penn State was starting its football season under a new head coach for the first time since 1966. For more than four decades, Joe Paterno was the face of the Penn State football program. However, Penn State endured a tumultuous end to the previous season, including Paterno's firing in the wake of the Jerry Sandusky scandal. Bill O'Brien was hired in the off-season to lead the Nittany Lions.

What they needed was to get the 2012 season off to a good start to put the difficulties of the previous year behind them. What they got was home opener loss to the Ohio Bobcats, letting an 11-point halftime lead slip away. The starting place kicker, Sam

Ficken, kicked two successful extra points... okay for his first outing as the starting place kicker.

Next they traveled to Charlotteville, Virginia to play against UVA, a game that many estimated should have been a reasonably easy win. The game hinged on field goals, and Ficken went one for five and made matters worse by missing an extra point. Penn State lost that game 17-16.

One news story summed up his performance, "Worst game I've ever seen of a kicker in my life. 1-5 on field goals. Missed a 20 yarder. Missed a 30-yard game winner. Missed a PAT. Pretty much missed every which way possible. And none of them were close either. All were instashanks." Similar stories abounded on sports pages and across the Internet.

DECISION POINT

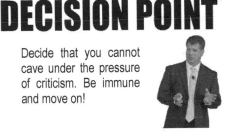

Decide that you cannot cave under the pressure of criticism. Be immune and move on!

But what was even worse was the firestorm that was unleashed on him via social media: "Don't come home, Ficken." "You suck, Sam." "How do you miss a PAT? Shoulda' been a gimme." "You cost us the game." And that's just scratching the surface. A lot of it is unprintable here, and a lot if it came from his peers... other students but not teammates!

These scathing comments were piled on a young man who was still a few months from his 20th birthday.

Did he buckle? Cave to the criticism? Quit? No. In an interview with *Fight On State.com* later that season, he said that it was "a little rough" on Twitter back then (referring to the post-UVA game comments), and then added, "I don't really care what people (think) who have no idea what my ability level is, and who don't really know me. All I need are my teammates, my coaches, my family and friends. I just didn't really pay any attention to it. It was out there, but you can't dwell on any of that."

Sam DECIDED to be immune to criticism. This young man DECIDED to be successful, and ended his career placing first in the Big Ten Conference for field goals made that year and fourth in the NCAA overall for the same statistic. He never missed an extra point in his last season, including the "walk off" game winner in the Pin Stripe Bowl. As I write this, Ficken is the leading NFL draft prospect for place kickers.

If a not-yet-twenty young man can stand up to very public, scathing, and far-reaching criticism, you can certainly follow his example and do the same. DECIDE to be immune to criticism and be successful instead!

Fear of Success

A fear of success can be just as real as a fear of failure. Maybe you worry about what people will think of you when you gain success and wealth. For some, the fear of success can be worse than the fear of failure. They fear the sustainability of success after they reach it, or they fear Impostor Syndrome (re-read that chapter if needed), believing that they really don't deserve success, no matter how hard they've worked for it. There can be a lot of guilt associated with the fear of success, and psychologically, the reaction is the same as the fear of failure. Like fear of failure, one of the components in the fear of success is worrying about what other people will think or say. Be immune to that.

Here is Coach Melanie's take on the topic:

Fear of Success

I've seen people really limit their success with this one. They're afraid that they're going to lose their life, or something else important in their life, if they become more successful. So it could be: "I'm afraid I'll lose my time freedom. I'm afraid that I'll lose respect from people. I'm afraid that I'll lose love from someone if I become more successful."

Imagine you have a rubber band around your waist and that the part of you that starts to become more successful starts to stretch the rubber band... stretch the rubber band... stretch the rubber band... and you stretch out to a certain degree. Then you're starting to make more money than you ever thought you could, and then you realize, "Oh my gosh, but what about John? What will he think if I'm more successful? I don't want my dad to be mad and think that I'm not loyal to him. I'm starting to worry. I'm going to lose my time. I've never been this happy. How can I possibly sustain this?"

Then all of a sudden the rubber band snaps back, and we're right back where we were. We've created this dynamic where we can't really grow because we haven't learned how to cut that rubber band.

Dr. Carri also shared with me her struggles with her own fear of success and what she did to DECIDE to get beyond that: "I've had a lot of head trash. But specifically, it's about my struggle with the fear of success. I've always been an introvert, like being alone, blending into the background, and like being a nobody. In order to grow my practice, I had to get over this. Writing my first book, I only had the concept and started having a paralyzing fear of success... afraid of all the things a successful book would bring: interviews, notoriety, publicity, etc. 'What if Oprah or Dr. Oz calls me?' I didn't even like the idea of more people looking at my website. It's crazy, but this is the reality of the fear-of-success head trash.

"This was stopping me from achieving my goal of writing my first book. I brought my fear of success to my mastermind group and could barely even talk about it. They helped me through it and told me I was normal and that they also struggled with this. Knowing that other entrepreneurs like me had the same fear was like a weight off my shoulders."

Opinions, Opinions Everywhere

There's no shortage of opinions. We all have them. Lots of 'em. There are a lot of people with no qualms about sharing their opinions, too… just ask Sam Ficken. Let me tell you something: There's only one opinion in the world that counts when it comes to running your business – your customer's… your **paying** customer's. Those people who are giving you money are the only ones who truly count. What they say matters, and that's what you should be listening to… that's also what you should DECIDE to listen to. Listening to the rest of the noise leads you to Squishyville.

Very often, our peers, our friends, our families, business associates, and the people we hang out with will share their opinions. These people probably don't understand how to run a business, and how to market a business, unless they're entrepreneurs themselves. They don't understand how and why you make the decisions you do, but that doesn't stop them from sharing their opinions about what you do or how you're going about doing it. Regarding Sam Ficken, I have no doubt that those who criticized couldn't kick a football ten yards.

You'll hear things like, "Oh, that's kind of ugly," "That doesn't make any sense," or "Hhhmmm. I'm not so sure that's really going to work for you." I've heard it all, and I DECIDED become immune to it. My business is successful. The people who make those kinds of comments don't really know or understand my approach. They're just forming their opinions, and they're certainly entitled to them. We all are. I simply don't put any stock in them. I nod politely, am immune to their criticism, and go on growing my Dream Business and living the life I want. That's exactly what you should be doing too.

Additionally, it doesn't help you or your business when you are with those who are critical. It stunts your growth to surround yourself with negativity, as Coach Melanie notes:

Success and Relationships

I think this is another element of mindset. I think the more successful we get, if our mindset is still in a weak state, we become very vulnerable to the influences of other people around us. We need to strengthen our inner game, so no matter what's going on around us, we're not reacting to that part of our world. We are responding and staying in alignment with whatever intention we've set for success.

This is one of the single, greatest problems for entrepreneurs because our business is so directly aligned with our performance. If we do not have the environment for success, like the friendships and communities we're surrounded with, we're going to struggle achieving success. If the vibration of our environment does not match the internal vibration that we're operating at (e.g. "I'm on fire, I'm going to keep moving, I've got massive stuff I want to accomplish"), we will, without realizing it, unconsciously bring ourselves down to match the vibration of the environment around us because there is a human condition that says, "I cannot be out of alignment with my environment."

To achieve optimum performance, you have to be in an environment that pulls you up to the next level. This is a new concept for a lot of entrepreneurs. The light bulb goes on and they think, "Oh, my gosh, I know when I'm around so and so, I feel like a train wreck afterwards. I feel as if they've sucked the life out of me. No wonder I have a hard time staying in motion." Some people unconsciously limit their focus and what they'll do because they don't want to "not fit in" with their friends.

It's about mentors, communities, support systems, teams that pull us up so that we are challenging ourselves to operate at a higher level of standards, a higher level of performance, a higher level of activity, a higher level of leveraged focus, where we're doing things so that there's minimal effort for a maximum result. That's when we're on fire.

Two-Step Filter

Over the years, I've developed what I call the two-step filter, and it's a skill or action step I want to share with you to help you become immune to criticism. This is something you develop internally, and you may have to work at it at first to hone the skill, but it's certainly worth your time and effort to do so. This filter is the best way to handle any criticism that comes your way. You know what I mean: When you hear something that's a criticism, a negative opinion, or a comment of some sort that gets your gut turning and starts to turn your brain inside out, and you start to think, "Uh-oh. This person doesn't like what I'm doing. I wonder if she's right?"

As soon as you hear yourself asking that sort of question and doubting your own judgment and ability, put the comment through the two-step filter. First, evaluate the person's expertise in the area in which she's providing the criticism or negative feedback. Let's say you've developed an ad for a direct mail campaign with a big flashy headline or some kind of unusual picture, and the comment is "Ooh. This won't work. No one will get this. You're making a big mistake. It's not good."

First, I want you to evaluate her expertise in direct mail marketing. Guess what? She doesn't have any. She's simply offering her opinion which, by her estimation, is accurate. I know otherwise, so I DECIDE to ignore her negative comments. Now if I heard that sort of comment from a colleague who I know is a direct marketing whiz, I'd pay attention. Otherwise, immunity it is.

The second part of the filter is to evaluate to what extent you trust and value the person who's making the criticism or the negative comment about your idea. If you do trust and value this person, if she's made constructive and worthwhile criticisms in the past, maybe you should take note. If not, it's time to put up your immunity wall. If what you hear comes from someone who's neither an expert nor someone you trust and value, it's just needless noise. It's the stuff that swirls around every day because everybody's got an opinion on just about everything.

Putting Up the Immunity Wall

Several years ago, I actually had a situation in which I had to really struggle to put up my immunity wall. It was shortly after I started my speaking career... you remember, the one I had previously convinced myself I didn't need, only to accept that if I wanted growth, speaking was a must.

DECISION POINT

Is your critic an expert? Does the opinion of your critic matter to you? No? Ignore it and move on!

You've probably noticed the caricature I use of myself at the start of each chapter. I also use that in other literature, newsletters, etc. To a degree, it's part of my brand.

So there I was, getting ready to deliver my speech and was about 30 to 60 seconds from taking the stage. I was standing off to one side while the host of the event introduced me. Projected on the screen during this introduction was my caricature. As I waited, some guy scurried up next to me and whispered, "Jim, I really find that cartoon of you quite disturbing."

I'll admit, my silent reaction was "Oh my gosh! Disturbing? I wonder how many other people think it's disturbing. Why didn't anybody tell me this before? Disturbing? What's disturbing about it?" I got discombobulated pretty quickly, and it was a real challenge for me to keep my head on straight and deliver my message. Not anymore. I have DECIDED to ignore the opinions of others every time I put myself out there. If I had honed the skill of applying the two-step filter at that time of the "disturbing" comment, I would have known that this guy was someone whose opinion I didn't value and was not someone who had earned my trust. If this scenario were to play out today, my response would be, "Thanks for your opinion. I'm getting ready to go on stage and share my expertise."

If you find yourself listening too closely to what other people are saying, start working on developing your own two-step filter. If what you're doing is working for you and working for your business, if you're bringing in more customers and growing, that's the only measure that matters. Develop a thick skin. Become immune to criticism and keep growing you Dream Business to live the lifestyle you want.

Pulling the Ultimate Success Trigger:

* ❖ *If you want to be successful and really grow your Dream Business, you simply cannot need approval from others. You must DECIDE to develop a thick skin.*
* ❖ *Listening to criticism and allowing it to alter your plans puts you on the road to Squishyville!*
* ❖ *Success and failure are not diametrically opposed. The roads to success and failure often overlap for a while. Don't immediately do an about-face when you fail.*
* ❖ *Fear of success is as stifling as fear of failure.*
* ❖ *To be successful, you cannot continually be in the company of nay-sayers. Surround yourself with like-minded, positive people.*
* ❖ *Use a two-step filter when you hear criticism. First ask yourself if the critic is an expert about which she is opining. Then ask yourself if her opinion really matters to you. If either answer is "no," be immune to the criticism.*

DECIDE:

Immunity to criticism is an integral factor in your success. Just because someone says it doesn't mean you have to act on it or even listen in the first place. Consider the source! Who is being critical, what is their expertise, does it really matter to you?

Do you want to be immune to criticism?

Pros:

_____

_____

_____

_____

Cons:

_____

_____

_____

_____

Yes, here is the action I will take:

_____

No, here is what I will do instead:

_____

Decide to Be Immune to Criticism

Chapter Eight:
Decide NOT to Be Perfect

Perfection is the enemy of progress.

I know several entrepreneurs who describe themselves as "former corporate types." What they mean by that is in the corporate world everything needs to be perfect before shown to a customer or implemented or marketed. And the level of perfection expected dictates the number of proofreaders and committees that need to sign off on something.

Of course, in the corporate world, another reason for perfection is that getting called to the boss's office is no fun after they (or one of their golfing buddies) spotted the missing comma in a 2,000 word document!

There is one place that may be perfect, and that's Squishyville, but remember: nothing happens in Squishyville. In this case, Squishyville residents suffer from perfection analysis paralysis. They are too worried about a mistake, and they are suffering from slow-to-no growth because of it.

When I started my business, I too suffered from the fear of making a mistake and being seen as a mistake-prone amateur not worthy of someone's business (how's that for some head trash!) until I heard an expression by marketing legend Dan Kennedy, "Good is good enough." So what does that mean? Is it a license to put out shoddy work? No!

I first heard this term in 2006 when I was beginning my new branding and positioning as The Newsletter Guru and launching my second business, No Hassle Newsletters. I've come to understand and totally appreciate this expression – and business philosophy – because it relieves overwhelm, and it also greatly accelerates your growth because, honestly, finding every last comma and poor grammar choice before launching puts a tremendous strain on forward progress, especially in the early years when you are doing it all.

Coach Melanie understands that besides creating slow-to-no growth, perfection leads to overwhelm. (See Decide to Be an Entrepreneur for Coach Melanie's explanation of the different overwhelm syndromes.) Running a business can be overwhelming, so let me take a bit of a quick sidebar to share her perspective on this very topic:

Different States of Overwhelm

You will be overwhelmed by different things depending on the stage at which your business is. At the start, there are things like your web presence, product design, etc. Once you get those things created and running smoothly, you'll hit the growth stage of overwhelm.

You start to recognize that your business is running pretty well and you've made a lot of success. Maybe you set your sights on hitting the million to billion range, and now there's another level of stress because you're looking at different types of funding to grow your business. You may be looking at bringing in people who own roles from which you need to extract yourself now. It can be overwhelming because you're facing a lot of new tactics and strategies that you have never used and need to learn.

Finally, there's the stage that focuses on the legacy side. Maybe you want to extract yourself from the business, exit, or sell, so you have to develop strategies for the process, so it's successful. You may be faced with the overwhelm of "How do I release the business I have and set out into the unknown to pursue my legacy?"

At each stage of growth, there is uncertainty and newness. Overwhelm kicks in when you're faced with things you don't know how to do. It's scary because you're someone who likes to feel confident and clear about the steps.

One of the things I learned a few years ago that has served me so well to help manage and conquer that overwhelm is to recognize that the tools, resources, and strategies I used to get where I am now will not be the same ones I use to get to the next level.

If I resist and try to keep growing with the same mindset, the same habits, the same ideas, it creates more overwhelm. If I understand that every time I'm going to grow, I also have to up-level my game, resources, support systems, and strategies, then overwhelm is minimized.

In looking at Melanie's different states of overwhelm, it's easy to see where thinking the need to be perfect at each stage will put right on the road to Squishyville. As I shared, that happened to me at the start, worrying about if my web site was perfect. Perhaps you're in the same boat, pouring over every detail of your marketing material. DECIDE to pull the trigger and move along. Once you're moving forward, you may get too caught up in the

DECISION POINT

Perfection usually costs you much more than you'll ever get back. There is a very limited ROI on perfection.

perfection of the job you do versus someone else. Let go! Re-read Decide to Delegate again if you need to.

Kelly Roach had a really similar experience: "When I was launching my business, I had a lot of the fear and self-doubt that new and even existing entrepreneurs have about the image of the business… and that all of the details are perfect. I spent six months in the process of getting my website launched. One day, I broke down in frustrated tears because of all the technical b.s. that wasn't making me any money, and I'd had enough. I decided to go out to call on clients and promote my business, website or no website, and got my first ten clients. The big lesson was that I wasted almost a year on all this technical stuff that I thought I needed, and ultimately, my first 50 clients never even visited my website."

Wow. That's really powerful! Stalling your success because of a quest for perfection can obviously happen at every stage of your business... even at the end. If you get too caught up in a quest for perfection when you are deciding to sell your business or move to your next adventure, you may miss the opportune time to exit your business.

Good is Good Enough

To me "Good is good enough" means that you always do your best work – create great content, write great books, shoot great videos, etc. and then you pull the trigger and implement and/or launch your work. I used to use a team of proofreaders and I still employ some today, but my mindset has shifted from the need to be perfect to someone who regularly and consistently puts out helpful and useful information... stuff that has real value. I'm know as someone who cranks out a ton of content every week, and I've become comfortable with the fact that when I produce such a large load of content, there WILL BE a mistake or two... and that is okay!

A mistake or two is not a deal breaker for 99.9 percent of your clients or prospects. To me, it's all about putting out great information that can help entrepreneurs grow a more profitable business faster, and it is not about me being a perfect writer, author or speaker.

There were two big events that helped me realize this seismic shift in thinking.

When I was launching the No Hassle Newsletter web site, I was running behind and had an unmovable launch date because I was exhibiting at a marketing conference. I knew the site was less than perfect, but I needed to board a plane and go – so for better or worse, it launched!

After the first day of exhibiting, I returned to my room exhausted and opened my laptop to look at the site. I started reading and was startled to see quite a few mistakes in the copy. Yikes! I did a thorough review, creating a Word doc of edits for my web site guy to make in the morning. When I finished, I opened email and saw seven orders from the web site. To say I smiled was an understatement. The bottom line was that I was making money online – spelling mistakes and all!

Again, I am not suggesting you do substandard work. To the contrary: Do your best work and then pull the trigger and makes corrections and edits as you move forward – making money!

The other big lesson for me came from Bill Glazer, past President of GKIC. I was about 18 months into writing my first book, *The Magic of Newsletter Marketing*, when I heard Bill speak on the topic of authoring a book. My book had technically been done for a few months and every chance I had I was proofreading it to find every last mistake and correct it. This was before Create Space where you can now make edits and upload new guts to a book on the fly – this was when you printed and shipped a garage full of books!

Bill was speaking about "good is good enough," and he happened to mention book writing. Here's what Bill said: "Just imagine you're in a book store and someone sees your book. Intrigued by the cover, they pull it off the shelf and thumb through it… and then buy it. For starters, you've made sale and it's possible that book sale will lead to other business. On the other hand, if your book is still in your computer while you look for every last grammar and spelling mistake – no sale and no future business."

I am grateful to Dan Kennedy and Bill Glazer for getting my head straight about this. I launched *Magic* later that month and the book you're holding is number six – and my average time to write a book is now three to five months!

Let me also point out that people will be more than happy to point out the mistakes you miss. I guarantee that will happen

DECISION POINT

A book on the shelf with a typo or misplaced comma is worth far more than the one in your head or on your computer.

because it happens to me more than a couple times a month. Some people get indignant and nasty – I have no clue why – but it can be off putting when you get the first one. When that happens, just say to yourself, "It's okay because they are probably not a good prospect for me anyway, and the amount of good content I put out more than makes up for the occasional gaffe."

I truly believe that, and it helps to say it out loud if someone rattles your cage. With today's technology and the flexibility it offers, correct the mistake they pointed out (whether on your site, a PDF document, etc.) and move on.

Dr. Michele Summers Colon is a great example of DECIDING to escape being mired in perfection and analysis paralysis: "I was stuck in perfection regarding sending out newsletters, so I stopped sending them. When I started with "No Hassle Newsletters," that really solved the problem, and I just don't worry about it anymore."

Plus Gary George shared an eye witness account of how perfection doesn't pay: "The first time I realized that I needed to do things faster and stop being a perfectionist was when I had two new clients who were both in the same industry but in different geographic locations. One was marketing and working more aggressively, and they were able to accomplish so much more than the other who was the perfectionist, going back to 'cross every t and dot every i.' I saw the first one do ten times the volume and become a multi-million-dollar business. The other ended up going out of business. I realized I needed to do the same thing and learn to let it go."

So the bottom line is: DECIDE to be a purveyor of great content. Generously share content across multiple platforms on a persistent and consistent basis and you will attract more customer and prospects to what you have to offer. Do not put out shoddy work; instead put out the best work you can and then pull the trigger and launch it. As Bill Glazer said, it does you and nobody else any good sitting in your computer.

I remember after writing my first book, I proudly gave copies to friends and family. One of our close friends is an exceptional writer and apparently proof reader! One day she told me how much she enjoyed my book but that it contained some grammar mistakes and even a "dangling participle" or two! I must admit I had heard the term somewhere but had no clue what it was. I would venture to say that the book you're reading right now has some mistakes – perhaps even a dangling participle – but there are three realties that I care about more:

1) *The content and information in this book is going to help other entrepreneurs grow more profitable businesses.*

2) *This book will help grow my business.*

3) *I never claimed to be a professional writer, and I have become immune to criticism. But the only way for me to share what I know about marketing and growing businesses with thousands of entrepreneurs was to write this book, and while I know it is not perfect, it is my best work!*

I'll close out this chapter with Susie Miller's comments about the challenges of worrying about perfection: "As a recovering perfectionist, the question about perfection hit home. In writing my book, there was always something more that could be done. I set a deadline and made it public, and I did that because someday never comes. The manuscript is in, and if I think I should have said something a bit differently or added a comma, it's too late. BUT, I will now have a book on the shelf.

"When I've taken the leap, not worried about perfection, I have more gratitudes than regrets."

Pulling the Ultimate Success Trigger:

- ❖ *Perfection, except in gymnastics or similar sports, doesn't pay. In business, perfection is the enemy of progress.*
- ❖ *"Good is good enough" doesn't mean shoddy or careless work, but it does relieve overwhelm and accelerate your growth.*
- ❖ *Considering the different states of overwhelm, each one presents the potential for slow-to-no growth by being stuck in perfection analysis paralysis.*
- ❖ *Accept that there will be a mistake or two. Fix it when you find it and move on.*
- ❖ *Content sitting in your computer waiting to be proofread again and again will never make you any money.*
- ❖ *Don't worry about people who point out your mistakes. As I said, fix them and move on.*

DECIDE:

Perfection stunts or completely stalls business growth. Accept that good truly is good enough, but don't confuse that with shoddy work... it's *good* work that is ultimately good enough.

Will you DECIDE not to be perfect?

Pros:

_____

_____

_____

_____

Cons:

_____

_____

_____

_____

Yes, here is the action I will take:

_____

No, here is what I will do instead:

_____

Chapter Nine:
Decide to Take the
Rewards of Risk and
Speed

One of my favorite expressions that relates to building a successful business is: "Wealth rewards risk, and wealth rewards speed."

So what does that mean and more importantly how can you use it to build your Dream Business?

First, it's important to shift your thinking from wanting to simply create "more sales" and instead move to wanting to create more wealth. (Re-read Decide to Be an Entrepreneur is you need a refresher on creating wealth instead of simply generating more sales.) Focusing on generating more sales rather wealth creation is leading you to Squishyville. The entrepreneurs who are living there, even temporarily, are risk adverse and slow.

Let's look at the difference between wealth and income, and I'll remind you about my earlier disclaimer about my complete lack of formal training in this area! I'm simply sharing my thoughts on the subject, and my approach has served me well.

Income or revenue is the measure of your compensation. It is how much money you exchange, or get paid, to provide a service or to sell your products. This can be referred to as the Gross – meaning gross revenue which is income before expenses.

Wealth is the sum of the value of your assets. This can include assets owned by your business and by you personally. Wealth is money already earned and saved and can be used by its owner.

Wealth brings you freedom.

Too many entrepreneurs focus most of their efforts solely on generating more sales. While high sales and consistent predictable cash flow can be liberating, I suggest your goal should be to grow a more profitable business faster, so that you can create more wealth.

Some entrepreneurs, particularly those in the Internet marketing space, like to throw around big numbers. Some may say, "I had a six-figure launch." That's clearly admirable, and I'm not diminishing the achievement, but wealth is not created from what you make (gross), it's created from what you keep.

I use an expression in my coaching business to illustrate this point, and I also display it at my Dream Business Academy events. "Gross is for Vanity – Net is for Sanity."

Gross is what people most often brag about. But net is what pays the bills, allows you to reinvest in your business, put away for retirement, bonus your team, give back to others, etc. If you gross a million but have expenses of $1,000,001, you're in the hole no matter how much you want to brag about that million dollar figure.

Okay, before I stray into waters in which I'm clearly not able to swim, let me get back to the main subject of risk and speed.

If you've ever been to Las Vegas, Atlantic City, or other gambling locales, you know that there is an inherent risk when you place a bet. When you invest in the stock market instead of placing your money in a regular saving account at your local bank, you do so hoping for a larger return (or reward) on your money. While the risk is less than that in a casino, there is more risk in the stock market than a savings account.

With those three examples you can see how the greater the risk, the great your chance of losing your money – but also, if it works out in your favor, the greater the reward.

It's like that for entrepreneurs also. Understand that everyone is wired differently and has been raised, schooled, and trained to be comfortable with varying levels of risk.

Entrepreneurial Risk Levels

Let's use the three examples I just mentioned.

Risk Level One – The Saving Account: This entrepreneur will start a business with no borrowed money with the intention that if it works, they'll reinvest part of the profits to grow the business over time. They might read and learn new marketing strategies but will usually do everything themselves to save money – and keep the risk low. Even when they become aware of the success and track record of certain strategies, such as attending seminars, joining a mastermind, or hiring someone with a skill set they don't have (perhaps copywriting or sales), they will usually not do so unless the business can afford it.

Risk Level Two – The Stock Market: As an analogy, this entrepreneur wants more of return than the paltry 0.5 percent a savings account pays, and they will take some of their money and invest in the stock market. In business, this means they're open to spending or even borrowing to grow their business faster. In essence, they're gambling on their future – or some may say, they're putting their money where their mouth is. When it comes to investing in faster growth, they are more open to using money they do not currently have in order to get the higher payoff. Clearly this is riskier than the savings account entrepreneur, but with calculated risks come larger rewards.

Risk Level Three – The Casino: This entrepreneur has a high tolerance for risk and an even higher level of confidence that basically says, "There's no way that I can lose; I'm in it to win it, and I insist on playing big or I'm going home." If you read about and study some of the most successful large brands and companies today, you will see most fit this profile: from Steve Jobs and Apple to Fred Smith and Federal Express. They gambled big and they both won big. In fact, with FedEx it was impossible to start a company that had jet planes without going all in and batting for the fences.

This perhaps overly simplistic view of entrepreneurial risk is designed to do one thing: Get you to open your eyes and think about where you are right now in your business. In my view, you

DECISION POINT

Decide that you cannot grow your business without taking risk, and the rewards are directly proportionate to the risk.

can be the most talented person at (fill in the blank with your skill set) but without the proper mindset about what it takes to build a highly successful business, you may not get there.

Let me share a little of my story as it relates to risk, and another of my 3:00 a.m. moments.

About five years into my business, when I was starting my transition to my current business model, I was still heavily in debt and doing my best to help provide for my family. I also recognized that in my mid-forties, I felt the time was beginning to grow short for me to create the kind of wealth Stephanie and I would need to prepare for retirement. I knew I had to play a big game and taking it slow and simply investing in my future growth based solely on cash flow (i.e. being a "savings account entrepreneur) was not going to get the job done.

Thankfully, with the help of some wonderful people in my life, my once strong ego and level of confidence was back, and I was ready for this challenge. I loved being an entrepreneur, and I wanted more than anything to be very successful.

So when it came time to invest even more in my business – this is code for borrowing more money – what help me make the decision to go further into debt was this: I knew in my heart and soul and in every fiber of my being that I was doing what I was supposed to be doing, and I knew with 100 percent confidence that what I offered was of immense value and could help other small business owners. I simply needed to become well-known and get myself in front of as many prospective customers as I could.

Two other things that changed for me in 2006:

1.   I became very comfortable that the end game, the result, was more important than me needing to be the one to **develop** the ideas or create the programs that ultimately succeeded. I was on a mission to create wealth by building a Dream Business, and I was totally open to any and all expertise I could learn and benefit from. Far too many **entrepreneurs feel the need to "put their stink on everything"** or make it their own. I had a healthy ego, but I was no longer going to be the impediment to my own growth. Where do you stand?

2.   I got comfortable with my relationship with money and more specifically debt. Much of this comes from my work with Coach Melanie. Instead of being so emotional about money, I began to see it as merely a tool. I even switched up my language – and instead of calling it credit card debt (which I always believed to be wrong), it became my line of credit! You'd be amazed at how simply reframing something can make a difference. At one point, I had multiple lines of credit with nearly every bank, and I used them to fund my aggressive growth plan.

It's also fair to say that anything worthwhile likely involves work and risk. I once heard best-selling author Guy Kawasaki say, "Being an entrepreneur is hard and that you have to 'suck it up!' If it was easy everyone would be successful and rich – it ain't easy!"

Once again, I'd like to share what a few Dream Business Mastermind members shared with me about their experiences with wealth rewarding risk. Brad Szollose said, "During dot com boom, my company K2 Design was still pretty traditional, creating posters, brochures, and typical print materials. My partner said, 'We have to become an Internet company,' and this was at a time when no one even knew what the Internet was. I had a lot of doubts and resistance because I thought it was taking a step backward. We were trying to sell it, and no one knew what we were talking about it. After about three or four months of trying to sell this idea called the World Wide Web, someone stood up and asked for a CD-ROM hybrid that would launch a proprietary browser to their website for the annual report.

"From that moment on, clients started to come to our door in droves. We had to move quickly, hustle, and market ourselves differently. We had to hire employees to stay on top of all the projects. We went from me and my partner to 60 employees in a year and a half."

Today Brad's company has the distinction of being the very first Dot Com Agency to go public on the NASDAQ.

Dr. Anthony Weinert also has experienced how wealth rewards risk: "When I first started my practice, I had a partner, but things didn't work out, so I had to start over with ambition and drive to make things happen. You have to have a main 'why' and purpose. My family was a big driver for me. If you have the 'why,' you can do whatever you set your heart on.

"Having a new building and zero patients was a big risk and also the impetus to do things quickly. There was a lot of dedication and legwork to get started. You need a lot of focus to strive to be the best."

I've mentioned it elsewhere in this book, but it bears repeating: Most small businesses fail within five years and 80 percent are gone in eight years. It is risky launching a small business. But the reward... if you do it correctly... can be huge. There is no better way to create wealth and stability than by becoming a successful entrepreneur.

To be clear, for every entrepreneur who risks everything to start a business, there are many who fail and lose everything. That is the risk associated with doing something other than showing up and cashing a paycheck.

In general, in life and business, the greater the risk, the greater the potential reward. I believe that. So when entrepreneurs want to play it safe, and not risk being bold or investing in their future business (buying speed) – they also cannot expect to have the same size reward as someone who is willing to risk more.

Wealth Rewards Speed

Now let's talk about the other side of reward – speed.

Entrepreneurs who get stuff done fast are much likelier to grow their business and achieve higher wealth.

I have been coaching other entrepreneurs for six years and I've seen folks who take a long time to create a blog and post to it regularly. Conversely, I've also seen entrepreneurs in the same time period create a blog, video series, podcasts, write a book and rebrand themselves. Guess which one is seeing higher profits? Guess which one is generating wealth?

To be fair, everyone has different circumstances and time constraints. However, I've also witnessed in my own business and those of many others the effect of bold action (risk) and being fast to implement (speed), and without fail, when more risk is appropriately used and fast implementation is involved, the chances of growing a more profitable business faster is greatly increased.

In order to reevaluate your ability to get stuff done fast, re-read the Decide NOT to Be Perfect chapter. My business mentor, Dan Kennedy says, "Success leaves a messy kitchen." This is true. When you're moving at a high rate of speed, you're going to create a mess. If you're okay with occasionally creating a mess, then grow your business full steam ahead!

When it comes to speed and getting lots of things done and implemented quickly, there are several strategies that you can use to actually make your life a lot easier. I teach many of them at Dream Business Academy, but I'll share one with you now.

We are all operating in content-driven environment. In the Internet world in which we live, content is still king. The fresher and more engaging content you create, the greater the chances are that more of your prospective customers will find you.

So how do you create a steady stream of content for your newsletter and social media? Well, I'd be remiss if I didn't plug two of my programs here, so let me suggest that you check out No Hassle Newsletters (www.NoHassleNewsletters.com) and No Hassle Social Media (www.NoHassleSocialMedia.com).

But I'll give you a tip that works great for me. It's called repurposing content. The idea is to create some content and then find multiple ways to re-use it over time and across multiple platforms. Whenever I write a book, the first thing I do is give it to an editor and have her take sections of the book and create multiple articles, blog posts, and Facebook status updates. One book can keep you in content for months, if not years. You may think this is akin to airing rerun after rerun, but here's the truth: not everyone reads everything.

Another strategy is to record a podcast and have each episode transcribed. The transcript can easily be edited into multiple blog posts and Facebook updates, of course linking each post to your podcast! Again keep in mind that your prospects are probably not seeing every post or update or may miss a podcast or two. Also keep in mind the advertising statistic that prospects need to hear or read your message about seven times before they act!

These strategies and so many more are part of what I call my "Million Dollar Platform on a Shoestring Budget," and I teach every step of it at my Dream Business Academy. Check out more details including the date and location of the next event at www.DreamBizAcademy.com.

Dr. Michele Summers Colon understands the need for speed and its reward: "During a pre-launch or preparing for a trade show, everything has to happen quickly. Plus, everything depends on everything else, and it's a huge undertaking, so you just have to do it in order to pull it off."

Susie Miller added this about wealth rewarding speed: "I remember having more questions than answers. I looked at my list and just decided to begin. If I did nothing, nothing would change. Who knew when or if I'd have the answers: 'When I figure it out versus I'm going to get started and go.' I decided to just go and let the rest fall into place. This allowed me to jump my coaching practice to the point where I had a six-month waiting list."

Pulling the Ultimate Success Trigger:

❖ *Focus on creating wealth more than on generating sales. Sales don't necessarily convert to wealth.*

❖ *Gross is for vanity; net is for sanity. Boosting that you grossed a million dollars doesn't mean a thing if your expenses were $1,000,001!*

❖ *Remember the three entrepreneurial risk levels: Savings Account, Stock Market, and Casino. Saving Account is a safe bet, but you'll have slow-to-no growth.*

❖ *Your ego and the need to be the only idea and program generator will be an impediment to your ability to grow wealth.*

❖ *Speed usually makes a mess. Don't worry about it because being quick to implement ideas and programs leads to wealth creation.*

❖ *A tip to be faster: re-purpose your content. It may feel like a rerun to you, but keep in mind that your prospects don't read everything you share.*

DECIDE:

Squishyville is full of entrepreneurs who are risk adverse and slow to take action. There's no wealth there, and there never will be. Your risk tolerance and entrepreneurial speed will dictate your ability to create wealth for yourself through your Dream Business.

Will you DECIDE to reap the rewards of risk and speed?

Pros:

_____

_____

_____

_____

Cons:

_____

_____

_____

_____

Yes, here is the action I will take:

_____

No, here is what I will do instead:

_____

Chapter Ten: Decide to Be an Entrepreneur

If you've watched my videos, listened to any of my podcasts, are part of my mastermind group, you've heard me refer to entrepreneurs and small business owners. I even use both terms in this book. It's important to understand that these terms are not interchangeable.

So, you might wonder, what's the difference? I think the difference has its foundation in mindset!

To start, a small business owner is a person who owns a business, be it a brick and mortar location or a home-based online entity. While entrepreneurs can and do own small businesses, there is a difference, and that difference has everything to do with how they think about their operation... their mindset.

Small business owners typically think that the way to grow their businesses is by selling more of whatever it is they sell, whether that is a product or a service. If they sell widgets, they want to sell as many widgets as possible, to the point of maxing out their capacity and to the point where they need to expand their location or warehouse more widgets.

If the small business owners offer a service, they want to build their client base to maximum capacity... to the point where they cannot take on new clients without adding staff to help provide the service. Perhaps they also increase their geographic territory and again, increase staff support.

On the opposite side is the entrepreneur. He doesn't have tunnel vision, focusing only on selling more of his core product or service as possible. The entrepreneur focuses on a bigger picture and on wealth creation. In other words, they are open to and desire multiple streams of revenue and are also open to exploring new ideas and services to offer current clients or new clients. Instead of singularly focusing on driving more sales, they're looking for ways to create wealth.

I'll use my own business experience as an example. When I started my first business, it was called Dynamic Communication, and my sole focus was writing and designing newsletters for corporations, Chambers of Commerce, associations, and nonprofits. Four years later, I had 25 clients and was making a nice living. I began to wonder how many more clients I could add as I was running out of time in the day, and I was determined at the time not to have employees. "Not to have employees" is the mindset of the small business owner, not the entrepreneur.

DECISION POINT

Decide to take the blinders off and be an entrepreneur. Grow your wealth, not just your sales.

I thought life was good until my wife asked me a question one night after dinner. It was an innocent question but one that actually rocked my world! She asked, "Jim, when are we going to go on vacation?" You see, it had been at least five years since we'd had a vacation, but when she asked me that question, my first thought was not, "How can we afford it?" Instead, my first thought was, "I can't go away; there's nobody to run my business!"

"Nobody to run my business" is the mindset of the small business owner, not the entrepreneur.

I hadn't created a business; I had created a job for myself. Granted, up until that realization and having escaped unemployment and being broke, that job was satisfactory. However, with my realization that my business was a job rather than an entrepreneurial endeavor, I knew I was at a dead end. I couldn't grow and I couldn't create greater wealth. I was maxed out and overwhelmed.

Coach Melanie has a lot to say about being overwhelmed in your business:

Entrepreneurial Overwhelm

Being an entrepreneur and being overwhelmed almost become synonymous. Most of us don't recognize the impact that is coming toward us every day with email, mail, phone calls, and the constant bombardment of things we should do. The next thing you know, many of us have a to-do list a gazillion miles long. We have no shortage of great ideas. We have a lot of things we want to accomplish and big goals.

Then there's a gap between where we are and where we want to be. Because it's new and because it feels really big, most people tend to focus on the chunks rather than the little things.

Through Neuro-Linguistic Programming (in which I'm certified), I've learned that our brains can only process five to seven pieces of information at any given time. Yet we are bombarded with over a million bytes of information in any give minute. If that doesn't provide perspective on why we're overwhelmed, nothing does.

What I found when I started my business in the first 18 months to two years was that I was constantly drowning in a sea of way too many things to accomplish that I didn't have the time (and sometimes the money) for. The cold hard facts are that when you're not accomplishing the right daily activities and not focused on the things that make you money and grow your business, you will not have the results you want. You cannot grow. You can stay where you are but can't grow unless you're willing to work 24 hours a day, seven days a week, and then try to squeeze in 20 more hours somewhere. It's impossible.

None of us ever dreamed about spending our days chained to a computer trying to get everything done. Our dream is to have the time and energetic freedom to do the things we love to do.

Overwhelm Syndromes

There are three syndromes that I've found affect a lot of entrepreneurs that lead to overwhelm or in some way inhibit growth.

The first is Bright, Shiny Objects Syndrome. It's about having absolutely no clue about what is and isn't important and what will and will not work. In my case, having no formula for decision making, I would jump at anything that made sense. I was spending a lot of money and time chasing things that never panned out, and that led me to be more depleted and even further from my goal.

Bright Shiny Object Syndrome is when we don't know what's important, so we chase everything and hope something lands. When starting a business, there is so much coming at you that you can be like a kid in a candy store. We don't initially develop the muscle or the discernment of really understanding, "Is this an idea worth putting into action because it has the right return on investment."

The second is Super-Hero Syndrome in which we run around like a chicken with its head cut off, trying to accomplish everything in record time. We set unrealistic expectations of ourselves and think because we have an idea and make a decision that we want it done next week, it can magically be done. We don't consider other expectations, priorities, and commitments we've already made.

Super-Hero Syndrome leads to burn-out of ourselves and usually those around us. To avoid it, we have to get a clear understanding how long things take and what it takes to get something done.

Finally, there's Job Syndrome, when we try to run our business like it's a job. We think like an employee rather than thinking like a CEO. We tend to think "It's my business, I have to get it done" rather than thinking "It's my business, I have to figure out the most powerful, most strategic, and most effective way to grow my business, take care of clients, and generate the results I want."

Those with Job Syndrome tend to think small, play small, and get small results.

Whew. I had experienced all of the overwhelm syndromes she describes, and once I realized I was in Job Syndrome, driven by Stephanie's simple question about taking a vacation, I decided I wanted to be an entrepreneur instead of a small business owner.

My first step was to figure out how to use leverage. How could I leverage my skill and talent writing and designing newsletters, but get paid by multiple clients instead of one at a time? After five years, I launched my second business, No Hassle Newsletters! Today I serve hundreds of clients in nine countries with my famous "Customer Loving Content[TM]" and ready-to-go newsletter templates.

Next, I was on the hunt for more and different ways to generate sales and create wealth, and the answers came from my own customers! Ready-to-go newsletters were great, but they shared with me their pain of getting their newsletters printed and mailed. My next step was The Newsletter Guru's Concierge Print and Mail on Demand Program, in which I print and mail thousands of newsletters for clients all over the country.

Step three was to add my Custom Article Generator, which is a program where I offer the skill and talent of my writers to write custom articles for my customers. This service keeps my writers busy, and since creating content is a never-ending struggle, my customers love the service.

I was now a full-fledged entrepreneur, but the desire for growth didn't end. With the rise of social media and its inherent challenges, five years later, I created and launched another popular marketing program, No Hassle Social Media. No Hassle Social Media is an amazing content program for entrepreneurs and small business owners who need a ton of content, articles, blog posts, and more, so they can keep feeding their "content is king" social media marketing machine.

I then launched No Hassle InfoGraphics Generator to offer custom Pinterest-style infographics to entrepreneurs who see the value in harnessing the amazing web traffic that Pinterest is currently creating.

I created Success Advantage Publishing to print my books and several information marketing products, and we're also starting to publish some books for my private coaching clients!

Finally, I've created my Dream Business Coaching program and the Dream Business Academy – two venues in which I teach other entrepreneurs about marketing and growing profitable businesses faster. (Learn more about these and my mastermind group by visiting www.GetJimPalmer.com.)

I could not have enjoyed this growth without making up my mind to be an entrepreneur rather than a small business owner and using leverage.

Using Leverage

You can only accomplish more when you learn to leverage. I was always asking, "How can I get something done with the least amount of my personal energy and effort but that will have the greatest output, so I'll be able to have the furthest impact with it?"

The obvious place for this is leveraging other people's time and talent: delegation. If you've ever tried to learn something that is not your strength and forcing yourself to try to learn it, that can overwhelm the crap out of you. Leverage your time by delegating more.

If you have other people who are helping you move forward, then you have an opportunity to focus on the things you do best, and have others focus on what they do best, so all of the tasks are getting done simultaneously rather than sequentially.

What I've learned is that I don't want to learn everything; I don't want to be responsible for getting everything done; I want to focus on the things I enjoy and do best. To do that, the one thing I had to learn was delegation. Delegation gets you out of "overwhelm."

It's time for you to DECIDE to be an entrepreneur rather than a small business owner if you really want to create your Dream Business and live the lifestyle that you want. If you choose to be a small business owner, accept the fact that you cannot achieve the success you are dreaming about. Change your mindset, use leverage, and start creating wealth. Using leverage keeps you out of Squishyville.

Pulling the Ultimate Success Trigger:

❖ *A small business owner thinks the only way to grow is to sell more of the products or services they offer. The problem is they max out and become overwhelmed.*

❖ *Conversely, the entrepreneur focuses on the bigger picture and looks for expanded products and services to offer and uses leverage to create wealth rather than simply increase existing sales.*

❖ *Ask yourself if you have truly created a business or if you've only created a job for yourself.*

❖ *Syndromes of overwhelm include Bright, Shiny Object Syndrome, Super-Hero Syndrome, and Job Syndrome. They each cause you to think small, play small, and achieve small results.*

❖ *Delegation gets you out of overwhelm, and learning to leverage other people's time and talents is the sign of being an entrepreneur rather than a small business owner.*

DECIDE:

Are you a small business owner or an entrepreneur? To be the latter, you must focus on the bigger picture of creating wealth rather than simply increasing sales. While increasing sales is a good thing, that alone will not get you where you want to go because you will max out your own time and energy.

Do you want to be a true entrepreneur?

Pros:

_____

_____

_____

_____

Cons:

_____

_____

_____

_____

Yes, here is the action I will take:

_____

No, here is what I will do instead:

_____

Chapter Eleven: Decide to Survive

There are four seasons each year: spring, summer, fall, and winter. Depending on where you live, there may not be much differentiation between them, or perhaps maybe you have rainy and dry seasons.

As an entrepreneur, you'll go through plenty of seasons as well. Depending on your product or service, you may have cyclical busy and slow seasons. Regardless, every business owner goes through seasons of growth and perhaps a season of want or struggle. If you are facing either of the latter two, it's tough. I know it's tough because I've been there.

I mentioned that a lot of the impetus for me to sit down and write this book came from the reactions I saw in the audiences at my Dream Business Academy programs. I openly share my own story at those events (and as I have been doing on these pages) because I think it's very important to understand that if you are facing a rough season, you are not alone.

I'm reminded of the recent story of Rob Konrad, former Miami Dolphins fullback, who fell off his small fishing boat nine miles from the Florida coast. A sudden wave knocked him overboard, and with his boat on autopilot, it motored out of reach. With no other boats in the area, his only choice for survival was to start swimming. The sun went down, sharks circled him, jellyfish stung him.

He prayed for helped and in an interview said, "I just said, 'Look, I'm not dying tonight and I'm going to make it to shore.'" At 4:30 a.m., after 16 hours of swimming, he reached Palm Beach.

Rob Konrad DECIDED to survive.

Your rough season might not be life threatening, but I know it certainly feels like it at times.

A Season of Crisis

Without a doubt, my own season of crisis occurred when I started my business in Oct. 2001... and it lasted a full year. In retrospect, I refer to that as my revenue-free year. I wasn't just bemoaning... I was full out groaning at times... a lot of times. When was my first client going to come? Despite that nagging worry, I was constantly busy because I was planting seeds the whole year.

I was attending Chamber of Commerce meetings and networking like I've never done before. I was doing some cold calling by phone and knocking on doors. I was doing everything I could think of to spread the word about my newsletter marketing business.

With hindsight being 20/20, if I'd known how those seeds were slowing growing roots beneath the proverbial soil and out of sight, it might have made those 12 months a little easier to bear. Looking back, I was like a farmer. I'd purchased this brand new farm, and I had to completely clear out the weeds, prepare the soil, and then started planting a lot of seeds.

I was actually nurturing those seeds by the networking actions and early business-building steps I was taking. Finally in the twelfth month, the crop ripened and I harvest my first client, who turned out to be a pretty big one, and from there, more harvests in pretty rapid succession, and I was off to the races.

During that first year, my season of crisis, every month, every week, and almost every day that went by I wondered: "When am I going to turn the corner? When am I going to get a client? When am I going to get some positive cash flow?" It was really tough.

I DECIDED to survive that year and all of its challenges. I kept telling myself that I wouldn't give up after the first month, second month, seventh month, eighth month. I'll be darned if I'll quit when I close to getting my first client. How ridiculous would that be? I knew in my heart that I was going to be successful because I set my mind to it. What I didn't know was when that success was going to blossom.

If you're in a season of struggle right now, I hope you can find a bit of solace in knowing that you are not alone. I went through it and shared the stories of many other entrepreneurs in my book that I co-authored with my great friend, Martin Howey, *It's Okay to Be Scared – But Never Give Up.*

If your current season is a tough one, keep planting seeds and doing everything you can do to produce a harvest in the future. Be like the farmer who keeps planting because he knows that he can't give up after a crop failure. He's got to start working to be ready for the next one.

If you're struggling right now, DECIDE to survive.

Pulling the Ultimate Success Trigger:

❖ *Your business will go through seasons, both good and bad.*

❖ *You can survive by making up your mind to do so. Your mindset will dictate your survival.*

❖ *When it seems like you are in a season of famine, keep planting seeds for growth, so you can ultimately experience a bumper crop.*

❖ *If you are facing a season of crisis, take a bit of solace in knowing that you are not alone!*

DECIDE:

Decide to survive. Even when things seem bleak, keep planting and nurturing seeds of growth for your business. Like the farmer, you have to continue to prepare for the harvest.

Will I DECIDE to survive?

Pros:

_____

_____

_____

_____

Cons:

_____

_____

_____

_____

Yes, here is the action I will take:

_____

No, here is what I will do instead:

_____

Chapter Twelve:
Decide to Change Your
Mindset

There are undeniably many components of success, and you already possess some of them or you wouldn't have ventured (or are seriously thinking of venturing) into creating your own business.

There are plenty of people who complain about the grind, about working for someone else, or corporate America. Since you're reading, I know you are a person who has done more than complain. You decided to employ your skills, talents, and work ethic to create your Dream Business and your dream lifestyle.

You know you have a skill and talent that can fill a need and a niche, so why shouldn't you be your own boss putting those assets to work for yourself rather than rather than putting profit into someone else's pocket? You know the effort it takes to launch a business, but you also know you have the personal work ethic you need.

Those three things – skill, talent, and work ethic – are definitely components of success. But I have some bad news: those three things will only carry you so far. There are countless entrepreneurs who employed those three components but still ended up with failing businesses. People who were extremely talented, had the right skill set, and worked incredible hours but who learned the hard way that those weren't enough to create success. Or they're now working ridiculous hours, barely eking out any profit, and are far from running their Dream Businesses and living their dream lifestyles. In fact, their dreams have become nightmares because their businesses have become anchors, preventing them from having the time to do what they want or derive any enjoyment from running their businesses.

Yes, you need skill, talent, and work ethic but you need more.

A Word about Mindset

I said this wasn't another book about mindset, and it isn't; however, mindset does play an important role in your success, so I want to touch on it and the importance of how your beliefs will shape your success.

From *The New Psycho-Cybernetics* by Maxwell Maltz and Dan S. Kennedy, consider this statement: "Human beings always act and feel and perform in accordance with what they imagine to be true about themselves and their environment... and ultimately experience appropriate results."

Without a doubt, your results are the product of your thoughts, and your thoughts drive your action or, in some cases, your inaction.

As my personal mindset coach, Melanie Benson Strick has taught me invaluable lessons about mindset, so I'll take a moment here to include her thoughts on mindset:

Mindset and Beliefs

First, let's define mindset as a combination of the thoughts, beliefs, and attitudes that you hold about your life, your business, and how much success you can create. If the strategy you're using isn't working at the level you want, I've found it's almost always the lack of the right mindset.

Your business becomes your greatest personal growth tool. We learn so much about ourselves and what we're capable of... and where we're holding ourselves back simply by looking at the results in our businesses. Every single result I've ever created, any client of mine ever created, or any person I've mentored along the way has created is directly correlated to what we believe is possible. That belief is directly proportionate to the specific set of stories we've collected over the years that have defined our view of the world and of what's possible.

Over time, we don't realize we are doing it. We run around and collect evidence in life and do everything we can on an unconscious level to keep ourselves in a homeostatic pattern that supports what we believe is possible. We study with people who mirror that belief; we surround ourselves with friends who, on some level, mirror that belief. We are literally an energetic equivalent on the outside of everything we believe is possible on the inside.

Most people on this planet are working ten times harder than they have to, but they have a belief that you have to work hard to create more success. I'm not saying success doesn't require hard work, but after we buy into that, we never stop doing it. So we don't ever explore how we could create more success without continuing to have our foot pressing the accelerator to the hundred-mile-an-hour speed. Mindset becomes a dictator of what we can create.

Are you working harder than you have to because of your mindset… because you believe that's what you have to do in order to be successful? Again, you need more than a solid work ethic in order to build the business you want and live the lifestyle you are dreaming about.

Mindset as Fuel

For success, there are two components that have to be in place. There has to an internal mindset that is causing you to be able to take the right actions. We might think of it as the fuel for the machine (our business) we're creating. Then there has to be an external strategy that's designed to achieve the level of success we want. What I've seen, having coached people for so long, is that if you have one without the other, it's like trying to walk on one leg. You will wobble. You will fall over all the time. It's very unstable. I like to look at your mindset as it's kind of like the inner workings of a machine. The external is how the machine comes together and actually works as a system.

In looking at it another way: Your skill and talent serve as the machine, and your mindset is the fuel that drives it. You can't have one without the other. The greatest level of skill and talent will just sit there if there's no fuel... no motivation or mindset. On the other hand, all the most positive mindset in the world can go nowhere unless it is supported by the ability to serve a need profitably and get things done.

Mindset and Negativity

There's also a mindset of hopelessness: "I don't know what to do, so I'm just going to give up." Those attitudes are directly relational to certain events and situations from which we formed a belief about who we're going to be on this planet. What we have to realize is that there is a direct correlation between our thoughts, the actions we take, and the results we have.

Let's say you're somebody who says, "I can't do it. This is too hard for me. There are too many steps. There are too many things going on. I don't want to figure it out. I don't want to do that." If that's your mantra ("life's too hard" or "things are too hard" or "I don't want to have to learn things"), you'll find you'll resist taking action.

That lack of action will result in your failure to achieve a particular outcome.

On the flip side, perhaps the person next to you has the attitude, "Well, if I don't know how to do it, I'm going to figure it out." That's his mindset. In this mindset, he's being shown a path where there are a lot of new things he has to learn, and he decides to figure it out or hire someone to figure it out. Now he's on track generate results.

I watch people who aren't achieving what they want or are stuck, and it's because they've literally been telling themselves, "I can't do that," and they've stopped trying to figure out how.

One of the biggest shifts I ever had was when I stopped telling myself, "I don't know how" or "I can't afford that." You see, "I can't afford that" is the single most limiting thought you can ever have. When you say "I can't afford that," you literally shut down any creative possibility of achieving what you want or what you need. So I learned to change my thinking about things that I wanted but didn't know how to get.

Instead of saying "I can't" or "I don't know how" or "I don't have it" or "I'm broke" or any of those limiting belief statements, I would ask, "What would have to happen for me to make this investment? What would have to happen, so I could have that? What would have to happen, so I could create this thing that I don't know how to create?" Now my brain goes into a discovery process. Now I'm in a creative-solution-oriented mode where I'm searching. My brain's trying to solve the problem of "Okay, we need money" or "Okay, we need a new helper" or "Okay, I don't know how to do this; I need to learn it." So you open up and you expand your possibilities rather than limit them.

Wow. That's powerful stuff and a lot of that is at the heart of my decision to write this book. I personally struggled with this early in my business as did Melanie, and I know from speaking with others at my Dream Business Academy that this strikes a real chord.

Pulling the Ultimate Success Trigger:

❖ *Your skill, talent, and work ethic will only take you so far. There are plenty of failed entrepreneurs who had those three components but failed in the mindset department.*

❖ *Your mindset as a combination of the thoughts, beliefs, and attitudes that you hold about your life, your business, and how much success you can create.*

❖ *We are literally an energetic equivalent on the outside of everything we believe is possible on the inside.*

❖ *Your skill, talent, and work ethic are the machine; your mindset is the fuel that runs it.*

❖ *"I can't afford that" is the single most limiting thought you can ever have. Rather than making that statement, turn it around and ask, "What do I need to do in order to have it?" By doing that, you are opening up your creativity and the possibilities.*

DECIDE:

Understanding mindset and the power, both positive and negative, it can have over your business and your life is important. However, mindset can be tricky, and we're often limited by our own perspectives. You can only see through your own eyes.

Because of that, it's beneficial to work with a coach – someone who has a broader perspective and who will keep you accountable.

Should I hire a mindset coach?

Pros:

_____

_____

_____

_____

Cons:

_____

_____

_____

_____

Yes, here is the action I will take:

_____

No, here is what I will do instead:

_____

Chapter Thirteen:
Decide to Be Profitable

First things first: profit is not a four-letter word. There are those who have a very negative view of big business, associating all of the ills of society with the profit that big business generates.

The truth is, every business, no matter what size it may be, needs to turn a profit in order to stay in business. Ironically, even not-for-profit organizations must actually raise more money than they spend on their programs in order to continue doing their good work. Of course, that overage is funneled back into the organization rather than into stockholder shares or any other bottom line entry, but they still have to raise more money than they spend, much like the entrepreneur has to have revenues that exceed expenses.

No matter what business you're in, you need to generate profit. I'm not talking about unscrupulous CEOs who become profiteering crooks, like Bernie Madoff, Jeff Skilling (former CEO of Enron), or other people who profited illegally from their ventures.

However, there are some people who have a "greedy SOB" mindset about any entrepreneur who turns a profit. The foundation of a successful business is the ability to turn a profit by solving problems and curing pains. Those problems and pains may be figurative, or they may be quite literal, as in the case of businesses that help people recover from disasters and catastrophes. Is it unfair for these types of businesses to turn a profit? Of course not. It's as fair for them to be profitable as it is for you to be profitable.

Take SERVPRO® – the fire and water damage restoration service – as a prime example. The company is in business to clean up after its clients suffer a catastrophe, like fire or flood damage.

Do they turn a profit as the result of someone else's very literal hardship? Yes. Is that wrong? Absolutely not. If they weren't profitable, they'd close up shop and wouldn't be there the next time someone suffered a catastrophe... leaving that person (possibly you) or business to attempt to clean up without the resources they need.

Similarly, have you ever had windshield damage? If so and if it wasn't covered by insurance, weren't you glad there was someone available to make the repair? Did they ease your problem of a smashed or damaged windshield? Did you begrudge that company making a profit? I suspect not.

DECISION POINT

Decide that profitability is not a four-letter word. Decide to be as profitable as you can be.

On the other side of the coin, alarm companies make their profit proactively. If the news wasn't filled with stories of break-ins and robberies, there would be no need for alarm companies. If you've ever been the victim of a break-in, you know how unsettling this crime can be. Your pain point becomes the worry that it could happen again. The alarm company you pay eases that pain by providing some peace of mind. Your alarm monitoring service is making money to eliminate, or at least, ease your worry. Is that wrong? I suspect you don't believe so... especially if you've had the unfortunate experience of being the victim of a robbery.

The same is true of exterminators and pest control companies. They ease the worry of ridding your house of bugs, vermin, and the diseases they may carry. Do they deserve to turn a profit? Yes.

Your Profitability

You're in business because you have a skill or talent that can solve someone else's problem. Because of that skill, you have the opportunity to create wealth for yourself by being profitable. There's nothing wrong with that. Without doing anything illegal, you have every right to charge what the market will bear for your service.

If you have extraordinary sales consulting skills and encounter a business owner who desperately needs to increase his sales, you are in a position to solve his problem. You may not think that problem is on the same level as the catastrophes of fires, floods, or burglaries, but that business owner who employs a staff of 20 and needs to make payroll probably sees it as a catastrophic problem in need of a real solution. If you can help him, I am certain he does not begrudge you making a profit.

Ever hear the story of the home heating repairman who was called in to fix a furnace? There was no heat in the house, and the temperatures were well below freezing. The lack of heat was a pain, if not a catastrophe, for the homeowner. The repair man came in, surveyed the situation, turned one screw, and handed the homeowner an invoice for $200. "$200?" the homeowner cried when he looked at the invoice. "But you only turned one screw!" With that, the repairman took back the invoice, adjusted it, and handed it back to the homeowner. Now it read: "Turning one screw: $1.00; knowing which screw to turn to provide a warm house: $199.00."

If you are agonizing about raising your rates, I would like to share what Dr. Carri Drzyzga, The Functional Medicine Doc, told me during our interview on this topic:

"I remember early on agonizing over raising my fees… small amounts, too. It created a lot of sleepless nights, and I felt guilty when patients pointed out that my rates had gone up. I felt like a failure because I'd been in business for so many years and was still struggling to support myself financially. In the end, it was a bunch of head trash. I finally overcame my fee issue by reading Dan Kennedy's *No B.S. Price Strategy*. It helped me understand why I should never discount or offer free consults.

"It also explained the concept of charging what you're worth. It wasn't new, but I struggled with this. The thing that changed it for me was becoming a published author. When I saw the printed copy of my book for the first time, I literally felt something shift. Now I could really charge what I'm worth. It made me unique. My prices went up across the board, and now if someone asks about a fee, I have to refer them to my assistant... I don't even know them!"

Gary George shared a similar experience on changing his mind about how much to charge: "There was a time when I didn't feel as comfortable charging clients for services that I had mastered because I had been doing them for so long. When I knew it would only take me an hour, I was only changing an hourly fee. Then I realized that it wasn't simply an hour, it was the years of experience and learning that I did to provide the service."

Just like the furnace repair guy!

Steve Graves, founder and president of Play-a-Round Golf also understands that money is always flowing and that it always flows toward value: "We're definitely comfortable with earning the most we can from as many as we can as long as we can. If someone (including me) has a problem with us earning all we can, then I simply ask them how long they want us to be in business. It's that simple.

Susie Miller shared that she is still working to overcome her own mindset about money: "I'm still in the process of overcoming it! I was raised in a middle-class family and the mindset set was that we were successful and that was enough. I realized that every dream of success starts with the person deciding to change their circumstances and not stay where they are. There's a great line from the movie, 'A Knight's Tale' in which the peasant squire decides to pursue glory and is told: 'Go and change your stars!' All successful people have a moment when they are going to change their stars. They decide they are no longer going to settle for what they thought was their place. We don't have to 'stay in our place'."

Business success depends on solving a problem, no matter how big or small outsiders may deem that problem to be. There are many people who see entrepreneurs as being opportunistic and simply profiting from other people's problems. In a nutshell, that's the way the world works. Concerning yourself with how others view turning a profit leads to Squishyville.

DECISION POINT

Go and change your stars!

Dr. Anthony Weinert had a really great nugget of information to share regarding being successful and profitable: "As you become more successful, you will have more enemies and deal with a lot of obstacles. Even friends and family can become a bit insecure about your increased success or level of wealth. You have to be confident in your success. I learned that the more money I have, the more I can help others, and that's also become a driver for me."

Dr. Michele Summers Colon, physician, yoga instructor, and founder of 34 Minute Shoes also shared her thoughts about attracting wealth: "At times, when I was earning significantly more, sometimes family and friends became uncomfortable and that caused me to be uncomfortable, so I did two things. One, I included circles of friends who were as successful, and two, I reminded myself that I worked really hard to get through school to get where I am and that I deserve it. I decided not to let other people's opinions about it matter."

As long as you play by the rules, don't cheat, operate your business with integrity, and pay your taxes, then by all means step up to the plate, launch your business, and solve other people's problems and cure their pain… and work to create a nice tidy profit for yourself.

To close this chapter, I want to share some really great nuggets from two authors who've written and speak extensively about wealth and the mindset that surrounds money. As you've already read, there are plenty of entrepreneurs who have head trash about money and wealth that are still resonating from lessons they learned growing up.

Maybe you're struggling with the same type of head trash, so I want you to really digest the following perspectives from two books that I highly recommend!

T. Harv Eker's Wealth Principles from *Secrets of the Millionaire Mind*:

- When the subconscious mind must choose between deeply rooted emotions and logic, emotions will almost always win.
- When you are complaining, you become a living, breathing "crap magnet."
- If your goal is to be comfortable, chances are you'll never get rich. But if your goal is to be rich, chances are you'll end up mighty comfortable.
- If you're not fully, totally, and truly committed to creating wealth, chances are you won't.
- You will be paid in direct proportion to the value you deliver according to the marketplace.
- Rich people focus on opportunities, poor people focus on obstacles.
- Rich people admire other rich and successful people, poor people resent rich and successful people.
- Rich people are willing to promote themselves and their value. Poor people think negatively about selling and promotion.
- A true warrior can "tame the cobra of fear."

Steve Siebold also has a lot to say about rich and poor, using the phrases middle class and world class in his book *How Rich People Think*:

- Middle class focuses on saving… world class focuses on earning.
- Middle class believes the road to riches is paved with formal education… world class believes the road to riches is paved with specific knowledge.
- Middle class worries about running out of money… world class thinks about how to make more money.
- Middle class think money is finite… world class see it as infinite.
- Middle class has a lottery mentality… world class has an action mentality.
- Middle class believes in financial scarcity… world class believes in financial abundance.
- Middle class waits for their ship to come in… world class builds their own ships.
- Middle class believes money is about status… world class believes money is about freedom.
- Middle class dreams of having enough to retire… world class dreams of having enough to impact the world.
- Middle class believes getting rich is outside of their control… world class knows that getting rich is an inside job.
- Middle class plays not to lose… world class swings for the fences.
- Middle class believes starting a business is risky… world class believes starting a business is the fastest road to wealth.

Pulling the Ultimate Success Trigger:

❖ *Never think of profit as a dirty word. Every business and even not-for-profit organizations must take in more money than they spend to continue their operations.*

❖ *The foundation of a successful business is the ability to turn a profit by solving problems and curing pains.*

❖ *Without doing anything illegal or unethical, you have every right to charge what the market will bear for your service.*

DECIDE:

Your ability to be profitable depends on your ability to solve a problem. As an entrepreneur, you may be hesitant to charge fairly for your services, thinking that you are taking advantage of your clients and the problems they face. Evaluate your pricing. Are you charging what you should be charging?

Should I increase my rates?

Pros:

_____

_____

_____

_____

Cons:

_____

_____

_____

_____

Yes, here is the action I will take:

_____

No, here is what I will do instead:

_____

Chapter Fourteen:
Decide to Emulate
Successful Entrepreneurs

Being successful is dependent on your mindset. William Jennings Bryan said, "Destiny is no matter of chance. It is a matter of choice. It is not a thing to be waited for; it is a thing to be achieved."

Your achievement depends on your mindset. If you don't believe you can succeed, you won't. It's that simple. Set your mind on succeeding and remember the old saying, "Success doesn't go to the stronger, faster man. Success goes to the one who believes he can."

In addition to mindset, there are common habits of highly successful entrepreneurs. I'm an early riser, and after I work out, I skim through a few web sites that I like to visit for inspiration. One morning, not long ago, I came across a great article on habits of highly successful entrepreneurs. The list included ten. At 7:30 in the morning, I'd already had five of them checked off for the day. I'm not saying that to boast. I'm saying this to share with you what habits you need to develop… habits that will help you emulate successful entrepreneurs. As it's said: Success leaves tracks. Follow those tracks rather than reinventing the wheel.

5 Habits to Create

I'm going to share these five habits, and they are in no particular order, but each will put you on the road to success rather than the road to Squishyville.

Habit #1: Get Up Early: Maybe you get up at 7:00 or event 6:00 in the morning. Let me tell you, that's not early. The successful folks and C-level executives typically get up at 5:00, 4:30, or even 4:00. For me, I'm usually working by 5:00, especially when I'm in massive action mode, like writing this book, launching a new webinar series, or planning my next Dream Business Academy.

A lot of times I wake up at 4:00, and boom... my mind engages and I start thinking about my business: "Don't forget to include this in the book; that would make a great chapter; what about the title; share these tips on my coaching call." At times, I say in that zone and simply let the creative process happen.

Getting up early is a way to get things done. It will probably also let you balance family time with fewer interruptions early in the morning and getting stuff done to have time at the other end of the day for your family.

DECISION POINT

Decide to create habits that will move your business and your life forward. Copy other successful entrepreneurs!

Habit #2: Exercise: Exercise is really, really important. It gets you going and creates energy, and energy begets energy. Want more of it to get through your day? Start with some exercise in the morning. For a lot of entrepreneurs, exercise frees their mind for greater creativity. A lot of my coaching clients have told me that they get some of their best ideas during a workout.

Habit #3: Brain Power: Feed your mind. Your brain is the world's greatest computer. What's true of computers is true of your brain: garbage in, garbage out. Focus on what's important. Spend your time on activities that feed your mind and power up your brain. Don't waste your time on pointless activities. Read books that make a difference. You know what sucks your time and wastes it... television, social media, email jokes. Feed your mind with positive things, and if you do it first thing in the morning, it sets a great tone for the rest of your day.

Habit #4: Express Gratitude: Being a man of faith, I always go to prayer first thing in the morning. I give thanks for all the blessings in my life, and I know I have blessings in my life, but I like to actually recount them. So, first of all, my health, my relationship with God, my wife, my children, my grandson, my home, my boat, my dog, my cat. I go through this whole list of things that I'm thankful for. I think simply doing that means that you've got a lot going on.

It doesn't matter what your faith may be. Recount all the things you're grateful for on a daily basis. Some people write in a journal and use that forum to express the things for which they're grateful, and I think that's great. Whatever it is, whatever you do, and however you recount them, be thankful for and actually recite, recount in your mind the things for which you're grateful... all the great things that are going on in your life.

Take it from someone who's been in a very, very, very, very low place. Even when you're in a low place, you can find things to be thankful for. At my worst when I was unemployed, heavily in debt, and fighting cancer, I had the most amazing support system starting with my wife, Stephanie, my children, my parents, everybody. I had this great support network. I still had a home. We never missed a meal. There are things that you can find to be grateful for even when you're in a tough spot.

Habit #5: Be Bold: DECIDE to take bold, decisive action. Don't think about adding one new client this week; think about adding ten new ones. I learned a lesson long ago about the power of zero: add a zero to whatever numeric goal you have. Not one client, ten; not ten blog posts, 100; not $100,000 in revenue, $1,000,000. If you're going to play, play big or go home.

Be decisive and DECIDE to take action. Make a plan, have a goal, make a decision, and then go act on it.

As with DECIDING to be different, there is a balance you must work for between taking a lot of action and avoiding the overwhelm that can result. Coach Melanie has her own formula for achieving this:

High Achievement vs. Optimal Achievement

We've mixed up what achieving means, and we think high achievers have to go at a hundred miles an hour all the time. I actually specialize in working with thought leaders and fast-paced entrepreneurs who are really creative and visionary. They realize they're working hard all the time but not getting any further ahead. They're running faster on the treadmill and they're staying in place, not going anywhere.

High achieving doesn't necessarily mean that you should continue to push yourself harder and harder and harder. What I truly believe is the success code, if you will, for life is recognizing what you want out of life and how well you're getting there. Most of us have a never-ending quest for more success. The whole reason I created my business wasn't so that I could keep pushing myself and working harder and harder all the time, making myself sick, debilitated, and exhausted. It was because I wanted to have freedom. I wanted to have financial freedom and I wanted time freedom.

I am one of the most successful entrepreneurs in my field. I've achieved a lot, but I also made a conscious decision to do it by putting my lifestyle first. So I wasn't going on this never-ending quest for more money and more success. I literally said, "This is what I want. This is what I want my life to be like. Who do I need to be to achieve that?"

I would look at ways to align myself with that success through leverage, though designing my business so it supported my lifestyle. And by simply looking at where I got mixed up about being a high achiever and focusing on optimum performance, because optimum performance really means that you know how to turn a machine on that generates success. That machine is you, your actions and the strategies that generate the success that you have right now. If you don't like that success, you've got to look at how to tweak the machine.

You can't get better results out of your strategies if you are not running the right program. Let's look at it like this: If you've got a Windows-based computer running XP, you're running really slowly. That's an ancient program. We've moved into Windows 8 or beyond. So if you have not necessarily kept upgrading your program with the level of your capacity, then you will feel like you're exhausted and you're trying to keep up all the time. I think that there is so much power that we can get out of our business when we shift the way we're playing the game internally, so that we can get better results externally.

Before you begin practicing habits of successful entrepreneurs, you have to first DECIDE and define what success means to you. That is your choice alone. Be clear on that or you may wind up compromising other important aspects of your life because you've allowed your business to take over the driver's seat. You have to stay behind the wheel to get where you really want to go.

Pulling the Ultimate Success Trigger:

❖ *Success goes to the people who believe they can achieve their dreams. You have to believe it first!*

❖ *Success leaves tracks. Study the habits of highly successful entrepreneurs and emulate what they've done.*

❖ *My five habits of success are getting up early, exercising, feeding my brain, expressing gratitude, and being bold. I believe those will work for you as well.*

❖ *There's a difference between high achievement and optimal achievement. Thinking that going 100 miles per hour all the time is high achievement is the quickest way to overwhelm and burn-out. Be an optimal achiever by letting the machine, your business, work for you... not the other way around.*

❖ *DECIDE what success means to you... not to your peers or anyone else. Only you can define your success and achieve it.*

DECIDE:

Don't reinvent the wheel. The path to success has already been blazed by others. Study highly successful people and learn what habits they used to achieve. Define what success means to you and then develop the habits that will get you there rather than leaving you on the road to Squishyville.

How will you define your success and create the habits you need to achieve it?

Pros:

_____

_____

_____

_____

Cons:

_____

_____

_____

_____

Yes, here is the action I will take:

_____

No, here is what I will do instead:

_____

Chapter Fifteen: Decide to Use GPS

I'd like to introduce you to a new GPS system, one that will help you get your business where you want it to be and one that will help you fully realize your Dream Business and achieve the lifestyle you want.

This GPS relies on the ability to make decisions, not a global positioning satellite. It is the system that some entrepreneurs use to turn any challenge or difficult situation into a home run. I know a lot of people who have increased their "batting average" by using this system. On the other hand, I've met and coached some entrepreneurs and small business owners who either struggle to make the right decisions or can't seem to take the leap to move their businesses forward.

This GPS system stands for Guts, Persistence, and Strategy.

Guts

There are two aspects of "guts." First is "guts" as in courage and the ability to make hard decisions. The second part of it is learning to trust your gut, your intuition. Squishyville is populated with gutless people.

Business owners face daily tough decisions and hard choices. It takes guts to run a business, and there are three stages of guts, or courage, in the life of any entrepreneur.

The first stage is simply having the guts to start a business. There are millions of "wanntrapreneurs" (people who dream about starting a business). But few of them actually have the guts to pull the trigger and start their businesses. There could be several reasons for this, including a lack of start-up funds, fear of failure, or, believe it or not, fear of success. The bottom line is that starting a business takes guts – a lot of guts.

When I started my business, I was full of excitement and enthusiasm. I spent weeks making decisions, planning, designing a logo (admittedly important but not the most important thing I could have been doing at the time!), and filling out paperwork and new business applications. Then I arrived at my first roadblock... the first time I had to really put skin in the game.

I was faced with a $50 application fee. Certainly this was not a lot of money (except that I was broke at the time), but up until this point, all of my actions had not required a monetary investment. Suddenly it became very real and very public. I needed guts because this investment represented the feeling of "no turning back now."

DECISION POINT

Decide to have guts to launch and run your business, and decide to trust your gut.

The second stage, when more guts are required, is during the lean start-up years. I'll admit that my first full year in business was what I now affectionately refer to as "revenue free"! That's a nice way of saying it took me 12 months to land my first customer. With a family to support, I had to find a way to avoid going further into debt if possible while keeping my entrepreneurial dream alive. That brought me to my next gutsy move: borrowing money to keep the business afloat.

For many entrepreneurs, and this may include you, this might mean borrowing against your credit cards. Using a credit card is a quick way to keep paying your bills, but it is also emotionally difficult for many people.

If you are in this situation now, know that I feel your pain and understand completely. I was there. Nobody likes credit card debt, and here are a few things that I did that got me over the mental hurdle, and sometimes, gut-wrenching anguish, of charging things like my mortgage and food on a credit card (two big no-nos according to many financial experts!) while I was working on establishing my business.

First, I stopped referring to it as "borrowing on my credit cards or credit card debt." I hated this feeling so much that I had to find a way to make it palatable. So I started to refer to each transaction as either drawing down my "business line of credit," or referring to the balance on each credit card as "a business loan." It's not uncommon for any business to have business loans, so I had several with various banks that chose to lend me money in the form of credit cards.

Secondly, I also knew two things in my gut: I DECIDED I was going to be very successful, and I was never going to be anyone's employee ever again. This decision made it easy for me to borrow what I needed as my company started to grow. In a way, getting my head straight about this cleared my conscience and moved my mindset from one of "Holy crap, I owe a lot on my credit cards" to "I am one step closer this week to turning the corner on this soon-to-be-very-successful business."

The third stage of "gutsy" arrives after your business has achieved some success and you evolve from a freewheeling, shoot-from-the-hip management style to that of a more seasoned business owner who is overseeing established systems and procedures. In this stage, entrepreneurs typically grow more conservative or perhaps even downright cautious when making business decisions.

There are two reasons for this. First, you now have increased responsibility through your business to your staff, your customers, and your family. Secondly, if you went through being broke, that struggle never leaves (ask anyone who grew up during the Great Depression), so you make more calculated decisions to ensure that you maintain success.

This conservative stage can stifle additional growth and make you unwilling to try new things. My advice: To the best of your ability, always be on the lookout for new growth opportunities, new revenue streams, and new ways to harness your creativity to combine your current knowledge and experience with your once youthful exuberance and "damn the torpedoes" entrepreneurial spirit with which you started.

Coach Melanie has a similar perspective on what I refer to as the three stages of guts:

Entrepreneurial Evolution

There are three evolutions in every business. The first one is the striving phase. We're really new in business, and there's a deep desire to get ahead. There's a vision that we're striving toward to get to the next level. There's so much that you're learning, you're trying to figure out what's going to make you money, what's going to work in the marketplace, what's the right marketing strategy. There's a lack of clarity. You might know what you want to do, but you don't know how you're going to do it. Striving mode has a lot of energy behind it, but it also becomes overwhelming from the uncertainly and not seeing progress fast enough.

The next phase is the drive phase. It happens once you learn how to make money with what you do. You think, "Woo-hoo, I know how to make money all right. I've got this thing working now!" You're on a roll, pedal to the metal to try to make up for how slowly things went before. It becomes overwhelming when you get caught up working 12 to 14 hours a day. You feel compelled to keep driving forward. Without a clear picture of what success means, you don't know when to stop. In this phase, you have to ask, "What's really important? What are the priorities? What's at stake?"

I had this happen in my own business and had more deadlines driving me than I could possibly keep up with. I realized I had lost touch with what was really important. I had gotten so caught up in the drive and the game and "what's next" that there was no end to what I wanted to achieve. There was no end in sight because it was never enough. The key is that you have to have something that's more important than the business... something bigger that you value and the life you dream about in order to get the overwhelm under control.

Finally, there's thrive mode. This is when you realize that there is a level at which you can have success and have a business where you feel like you are in the flow. You don't constantly feel like you're pushing huge boulders up a mountain by yourself. You have made a decision that you will feel fulfilled and in flow with your business. It's almost like everything re-prioritizes. It comes down to making a decision about what's possible, followed by an updated strategy, more leverage, more automation, and a shift in your mindset.

More on "Guts"

The second part of "guts" is learning to trust your intuition. Whether you call it your gut, intuition, the universe, providence, the Holy Spirit, or whatever term you want to use, as an entrepreneur you should trust it. When I look back on decisions or plans that didn't go well, truth be told, my gut was "buzzing like a disturbed beehive," warning me not to proceed. However, my heart was saying, "Ignore that old conservative gut and plow full steam ahead, you brave entrepreneur!" Of course, I should have listened to my gut.

Whether it's a major decision or even one as seemingly simple as taking on a new client, pause and check in with yourself about whether it feels right, and you will likely get the right answer. Also remember Melanie's Green Light Formula from the Decide to be Authentic chapter and ask these three questions at every decision point:

- How is it going to get me to my ultimate goal?
- How will this make me money?

- What will I be saying 'no' to if I say 'yes' to this?

The hard part for many entrepreneurs, especially in the early stages of business is that we want a new client so badly, we often overlook the waving red flags, focusing only on the potential new cash flow. We ignore the nagging "seems too good to be true" that our guts are telling us. Invariably, the red flags are accurate, the client never orders as much as promised, never pays on time, and saps too many of our mental... and sometimes financial resources.

So the bottom line is this: DECIDE to trust you gut.

Persistence

The next part of your business GPS is Persistence. Nothing is more essential than the willingness to be persistent and keep going, even in your darkest hour. This is true in any endeavor, but it is especially true when launching and running your business.

The book, *Three Feet from Gold*, by Sharon Lector and Greg Reid, really drives this point home, and it's a book I recommend because I can really relate to this powerful lesson. I lived it.

Imagine if, after my first 11 months in business and not getting one paying client in that time, I gave up, refusing to tap one more credit card to make it one more week. Those were dark days to be sure, but what I didn't know was that I was very close to getting not just my first client but several more as well. All the seeds I had been planting for 11 months were getting ready to sprout. I hate to think about where I might be if I had quit. Certainly, I would not have the successful businesses I have today, so my strong advice to you is: DECIDE not to quit!

Being a man of faith, I also believe that God is constantly testing us. During those initial dark days of my business, I kept imagining God saying to me, "I'm not sure you really want this bad enough, Jim. Show me that you have the persistence to keep working, keep making one more phone call, to keep going to one more network event... prove it to me."

If you need more inspiration about being persistent in the face of adversity, I also recommend *It's Okay To Be Scared But Never Give Up*, the book I co-authored with Martin Howey. In addition to our stories, you can read the stories of nine other highly successful business owners and the challenges they faced and how they overcame them.

Strategy

Finally, the last part of business GPS is strategy. No matter what your business may be, whether you sell a product or service, it is essential that you have a clear and focused strategy for success.

Step one in creating a strategy is to have a business plan. Those words, "business plan," strike fear in the hearts of many new entrepreneurs because business plans seem complicated and difficult. A business plan doesn't have to be either one of those things – you can find plenty of templates and how-to information with a basic Internet search. The point is you really do need a business plan.

By going through the process of creating a business plan, you'll be able to see where your weaknesses may be and who your competition may be so that you can correct those issues before you even get started. You can also delineate opportunities and threats, taking advantage of the former and avoiding the latter.

Your target audience is another critical component of your business plan. Knowing exactly who your target audience is and knowing your market are more important than the product you sell or the service you offer. Please re-read that sentence: **Knowing exactly who your target audience is and knowing your market are more important than the product you sell or the service you offer.**

Don't skimp over this aspect of building your business plan. You want to know with intense hyper-clarity and specificity who your perfect target customer is. You should know how old they are, their gender, their occupation, the type of neighborhood they live in. Why? If you don't know this information, you will never reach them with any type of marketing you do.

All great marketing should be one-to-one communication. We all want to be special and be the center of attention. Your clients want to be the focus of your message. That won't happen if you handle your marketing (whether you're writing copy, shooting videos, tweeting, or posting on social media) as if you are addressing everyone on your list at the same time, whether your list contains 100 or 100,000 names. Target the message to a single individual – the right individual. And you can only know who the right individual is if you've done your homework and truly know your market. Be certain you nail down that critical information while developing your business plan.

Planning your strategy also goes well beyond having a business plan. Planning is integral to success, and one of the easiest ways to plan is to reverse engineer the process.

Reverse Engineering

The fastest way to sabotage results is by failing to have a plan. A lot of entrepreneurs don't do it; they think planning is not fun, not sexy, doesn't make them any money, so they by-pass it. I'm not talking about a business plan but rather a simple model to take your idea and put structure around it.

Reverse engineering means you think about what you want the idea to look and feel like at the end. Then you turn around and walk backward figuring out the pieces needed to make it happen.

Taking the time to do this upfront, to slow down and really think about it and plan it out does three things: It saves money (no need to pay a premium to expedite something you forgot), it saves time, and it helps you to know how to get there.

You have to start with the end in mind saying, "Here's what it needs to looks like and here are the tools needed to create it."

Keep in mind that there is no single tool to reverse engineer an idea that works for everyone. I'm a list person and work best in lists, so I'll map out all the lists and all the tasks in list formats. If you work better in pictures, a mind map might be the best process for you to work out all the different pieces, chunks, tasks, and activities. Some people are brainstormers who get all the ideas on sticky notes and then re-arrange them. Choose the tool that works best for you, but get it out of your head and into a plan.

The most important thing about your business plan or any strategic plan that you reverse engineer is that it should be dynamic. Your business plan should not something that you'll create, refer to in the initial days of your business, and then shove in a drawer or into a computer folder and forget about it. Similarly, you have to be flexible with other plans you develop to reach your objectives. Things don't always unfold or go the way we plan. Flexibility and the ability to alter course as needed will help you reach your target. Failure to plan leads to... you guessed it: Squishyville.

So now it's time to DECIDE to use GPS – guts, persistence, and strategy – and start moving toward success.

Pulling the Ultimate Success Trigger:

❖ *You need guts to launch a business. Once you do, DECIDE to have the guts to stick to your dream and keep going.*

❖ *Consider the approach I used regarding facing credit card debt and viewing it as a loan needed for me to launch my business. That mindset about debt may not be right for everyone, but I would not be where I am today if I had not adopted that thinking.*

❖ *As your business begins to thrive, do not become too conservative or you may miss opportunities to grow and prosper to an even greater degree.*

❖ *Trust your intuition and listen to your gut. It will be accurate 99 percent of the time.*

❖ *Persistence pays off. You will never know how close you are to building your Dream Business and achieving what you want if you quit.*

❖ *Planning pays off. You need a business plan and a strategic plan to reach your goals and attain your objectives.*

DECIDE:

Business GPS relies on your ability to make decisions and has proven to be the right success formula for many entrepreneurs. I faced many financial challenges when I launched my business, so I understand the difficulties intuitively. Now it's time for you to decide.

What guts, strategy, and perseverance do I need to create my Dream Business?

Pros:

_____

_____

_____

_____

Cons:

_____

_____

_____

_____

Yes, here is the action I will take:

_____

No, here is what I will do instead:

_____

Chapter Sixteen: Decide to Think Big

As I shared earlier, I had a problem with a narrow mindset when I first started my business. I'm forever grateful to have met a successful entrepreneur who took me under his wing and was my mentor when I was first starting.

At lunch one day, he asked, "Hey Palmer, what's your dream? What are you going to do with this thing you called Dynamic Communication? What's your vision for Dynamic?"

My answer: "Well John, it's very simple. I'm creating a business that's going to generate $50,000 in revenue, and man, I'm just going to be so happy." I answered with pride because I was only three or four months into my efforts and was thrilled at the prospect of running my own business. I now had real income after over a year of unemployment, and I knew that if I could earn $50,000 in revenue, that would be pretty cool.

You can imagine my surprise when John took me to task and, pardon the expression, bitch-slapped me across the table. His retort: "Jim, what the hell? $50,000? That's ridiculous. What's wrong with $150,000? What's wrong with a half million dollars? Jim, that's ridiculous. That is SO small time."

Yikes! I didn't realize it at the time, but that answer landed me in Squishyville. I could feel my embarrassment accelerating, but at the same time, I learned the important lesson of thinking big.

I've had any number of coaching clients who, when I pushed them to think bigger in setting their goals, question the wisdom of a goal that, in their minds, is neither realistic nor attainable, two of the attributes of the SMART goal system (specific, measurable, attainable, realistic, and tangible).

I can't speak to what any of them or you might be able to achieve, but I am very familiar with the power of mindset and the limitations our brains place on us when we let them. We need to flip that thinking around and let our brains figure out how to achieve our goals.

Let Your Brain Do the Work

Your subconscious mind has the answers. Let it go to work for you. The idea of asking a question about how to solve a problem you face before going to bed and waking with the solution isn't anecdotal. There is plenty of research that supports the power of the subconscious mind.

DECISION POINT

Decide to use the "Power of Zero" when setting your goals. Add a zero (or two) and think big!

The human brain is an amazing thing, and it can do amazing things when you let it. You simply have to get out of its way by eliminating small thinking and a narrow mindset. John kept pushing me to create a bigger business than I thought possible. I certainly didn't have all the answers or even a clue when he first challenged me, but I gave my brain free rein to brew on the problem of growing my business and coming up with some ideas.

Let's say you're in the business of making and selling quilts. Between the designing, cutting, and stitching, you can turn out and sell one quilt a week. Now I'm going to challenge you and tell you that you have to sell ten quilts every week. Don't resist and tell me it's impossible for you to make and sell ten quilts every week. That's knee-jerk-reaction small thinking. Instead, I want you to let your subconscious mind start mulling over the problem of how to make ten quilts a week and start feeding you the answers. It may not come instantly, and in fact, it probably won't. The ideas that hold the answer may come while you're sleeping, while you're driving, or while you're exercising.

Suddenly you realize that you don't have to be the chief sewer of quilts. You could hire other people to make the quilts according to your designs and your specifications. The reality is that you are not going to have a $1 million business or even a $100,000 business if you are the chief sewer of quilts selling one per week… unless of course you are selling them for $20,000 each. You might start out in your business as the chief quilt sewer, but I would love to see you transition yourself into becoming the chief marketer of your incredibly successful quilt-making business.

Steve Graves shared this with me when we discussed the power of the subconscious mind: "Worry is detrimental to growth, but meditating on problems can lead to progress. I have a quiet time each morning that includes scripture reading, devotional (*My Utmost for His Highest* among others), and prayer over our business problems. I generally describe our problems in a journal, listen for His leading, and write down what I hear. Over the last ten years, I've gotten many more ideas than I could ever put into place. I often go back over my journals to see what else I haven't put into place."

Don't let your preconceived notions (re-read Decide to Roll with It if you need to) and narrow mindset derail your opportunities for success. Dream big and think big, then let your brain do the work to figure out how to make your dream come true.

Leverage Leapfrogging

From the time we're born, we're conditioned to believe in taking things one step at a time. We progress through school linearly – grade one, grade two, etc. Every set of instructions comes with step one, step two, step three, etc.

It doesn't have to be that way. You don't have to climb the ladder one rung at a time. You can achieve more and reach greater success by leapfrogging. Don't be afraid to jump over different steps. Granted, this may not work if you're assembling Ikea furniture, but you're not. You're working on creating your Dream

Business and the lifestyle you want. It's perfectly okay to be non-linear!

Get ready, get psyched then go from step one and leap over spots two, three, and four, and land on five. It's like the old kids' board game of Chutes and Ladders. Maybe you remember playing it. It was really very simple. The ladders went up and the chutes went down. When you landed at the base of a ladder, up you went. Maybe it was only a single level, but many times it was multiple levels and put you closer to the finish line. Of course, on the other hand, when you landed at the top of a chute, you went down, and there were a few places on the board where you went all the way down.

Think about your business like a game of Chutes and Ladders. You want to try to leapfrog levels to become as profitable as possible as soon as possible. Sure, you are going to land on some metaphorical chutes. When that happens, maybe you scream. But pick yourself up, brush yourself off, and start climbing again. Of course, unlike in the game, you can use what you learned to avoid the chutes in the future.

DECIDE to leapfrog and take your chances with the occasional chute. You will be more successful faster.

Pulling the Ultimate Success Trigger:

- ❖ *Think big. Set a goal and then make it bigger!*
- ❖ *Don't get caught up in the idea that your goals should be attainable and realistic. That thinking automatically limits your mindset. Set a huge goal. You may not reach it but you'll get a lot further than if you set an "attainable, realistic" one.*
- ❖ *Let your subconscious do the work. Your brain is always working on a solution. Get out of its way and it will do its job. Don't stifle it with a narrow mindset.*

❖ *You don't have to take things in order. Learn to leverage leapfrogging to create your Dream Business faster.*

DECIDE:

Imagine that you're aiming for an "attainable" target. Chances are you'll hit it, but if you aim higher, your arrow will ultimately go farther! Small thinking lands you in Squishyville. Thinking big puts you on the road to success.

What will you DECIDE to do to let your subconscious mind solve your problems and how will you leapfrog your business?

Pros:

_____
_____
_____
_____

Cons:

_____
_____
_____
_____

Yes, here is the action I will take:

_____

No, here is what I will do instead:

_____

Chapter Seventeen:
Decide to Be Different

I've had several coaching clients tell me that they often feel bad because they can never turn off their ideas about their businesses and never turn off the entrepreneurial mindset. You may be facing the same challenge: Can't turn it off at night, on weekends, or even during time with your family.

In some way, you are always thinking about the business and wondering, "Why can't I ever turn it off?" You may wonder if this is leading you down the path to Squishyville. Actually, it's not.

I also worried about the amount of time I spent thinking about my business until I finally came to the realization that entrepreneurs are different. Look at it this way: When you are an employee, a nine-to-five person, you get to go home at the end of the day, you pretty much get to "check out" of work. Admittedly, the technology changes are linking more and more employees to their companies via constant email access, and of course there are some professions that require on-call status like firefighters, doctors, IT technicians, etc. As a regular employee, you get to leave and the business keeps running.

However, when you're an entrepreneur, owning your own business, it's always on your mind. That's the first part of it. The second part is that the line between your business and play… between fun time and work time… is very blurred. I don't know of too many entrepreneurs who don't completely enjoy what they do, so it's not like "work" at all. Most of them find it fun to create new ideas and think about ways to grow their businesses.

Of course there are challenges, but I'm not talking about them at the moment. I'm talking about how exciting it is to be an entrepreneur, so the line between work and play is blurry if not downright nonexistent. It's quite okay for you to DECIDE to be different.

The line is also blurred because as the business owner, you can create your own hours. That's one of the huge benefits! Not too long ago, Stephanie and I drove to the Chesapeake to check on our new boat, and then drove on to Annapolis, a town we love. We had really great seafood and made a fun day of it. Granted, during the times on the drive in which we weren't talking, I admit I was thinking about my next Dream Business Academy that was coming up, and that's fun for me. The bottom line here is that I can take a day away from my business whenever I want and can mix time off with some time to think as well.

Creating a Balancing Act

Although thinking about your business may be fun and exciting, you also need to create some real balance. You have make time for your family and other activities. Keep your priorities in order. Stepping away from your business (at least mentally) for set times does have its benefits. Coach Melanie has a lot to say about that!

Recharge

When you're working every day, you cannot recharge. Take some time away on the weekend. Of course, we're flexible. Another thing is have a lunch. Don't eat at your desk. You recharge your brain even if it's for a half hour. It's amazing what's going to happen for you. Your brain, your mind actually works a hundred times better when it's had space away from thinking about work. So oftentimes when I eat lunch, I'll go for a walk with the dog, or I'll read something inspiring over lunch. I'll just get my brain off work and just really reconnect to something that energizes me.

One of the ways that you can create more energy and more space is to plan your work and work your plan.

I have every one of my clients create a plan for how much money they want to make, and I work with them to reverse engineer exactly how they're going to get there. Then they work the plan. Interestingly enough, they waste less time because they're not sitting there spinning their wheels wondering what to do next.

It doesn't mean that you don't have flexibility and space to be creative. It just means that you really know how to be productive and use your time and invest it wisely in your business.

Creating Space

To really thrive, you have to create space. By that I mean adopting the philosophy that you make a rule and set standards around the hours and days that you'll work. A lot of people think, "There is no way in the world that is going to work for me." However, you actually become more productive and efficient with the time you set as your working hours.

For me, I don't work on the weekend, and I'm pretty much done between five and six every day. I don't get into my office before 8:30 or 9:00 in the morning, and I typically don't start working on Mondays until afternoon and most of the time I don't work Friday afternoons. If I work on the weekend, it's because I need a quiet space to finish a project. Thriving to me means I have the flexibility to work when I want to work and not to work when I don't.

Start blocking time away from your business. When you have time away from it, your brain works better; it has more energy. You focus better, you make better decisions. You're sharper; your game is at a whole other level because your brain cells aren't so deteriorated from working long hours.

You might love what you do, but if you're not taking a break, I guarantee you're not as sharp and not on top of your game as you could be. Take a real lunch instead of eating a sandwich at your desk, cramming more work in. Take a break, take a breather and get away for a half hour or hour, and your brain works better when you return.

So in the words of Ben Franklin, "All things in moderation." Although you can be different by being an entrepreneur, and thinking about your business may be as fun for you as it is for me, there does need to be planned time away, or you may become overwhelmed. As Coach Melanie also explains, you can take creativity too far:

Creativity Addiction

Every business owner I know, every entrepreneur, and every person who is at any stage of developing a business really prides themselves on being creative. It's almost like entrepreneurism and creativity go hand in hand. However, many of us are over-relying on the strength of being creative, and as the adage goes, "Strength overuse becomes our greatest weakness."

Here's what I mean by creativity addiction: You get so excited about the experience of creating something new that you spend too much time in the creation phase and never leave enough time to optimize what you've already made. For example, you think, "I've want to create another offer" or "I want to write another book" or "I'm going to promote another coaching program"; however, you're not leveraging all the hard work you already put into the most expensive part which is the creation.

Failing to do that leads to overwhelm because you're spending all your time and energy creating new stuff, but it never becomes fully monetized in the marketplace. I felt pressured to get new stuff out, and I realized that none of it was making very much money and wondered what was wrong. It's very difficult to be in creation and optimization mode at the same time. We get caught up in the new at the expense of making what we already have work better.

Creative addiction becomes your biggest weakness because it erodes your profits, creates overwhelm for you, and it leads to confusion about your brand in the marketplace.

The lesson is relax, you're an entrepreneur. DECIDE to accept that you are different. Be creative, but don't get stuck in the creative phase – you need to allow time and energy for implementation. Make some priorities with you family, but sometimes no matter when it is, you're going to be thinking about your business because it's fun, because we relish it, because it's ours. So enjoy being an entrepreneur.

Pulling the Ultimate Success Trigger:

- ❖ *One of the entrepreneurial challenges is thinking about your business a lot... but that's okay as long as it's creative thinking and not worry. Creative thinking leads to success. Worry leads to Squishyville.*
- ❖ *For most entrepreneurs, thinking about new ideas for their businesses and ways to grow is fun, and that blurs the line between work time and play time.*
- ❖ *As the business owner, you get to choose when you want to physically be in your business and when you want to be away from it. That is a huge benefit of entrepreneurship. Take advantage of it.*

❖ *Don't overlook the need to create balance. You must take time to recharge, and doing so will open your mind to solutions to problems your may be having or simply refresh you.*

❖ *Create space and block some time away from your business... no matter how much you love it.*

❖ *Don't become a victim of creativity addiction. Creating new ideas and programs may be a lot of fun, but if you don't allow time and energy to implement them, they'll never make you any money.*

DECIDE:

You may find yourself always thinking about your business. As an employee, you clocked out each day and the company went on without you. That's no longer the case. Accept that you are an entrepreneur. Fighting that may stunt some great ideas and lead you to Squishyville.

Will you DECIDE to accept being different as an entrepreneur?

Pros:

_____

_____

_____

_____

Cons:

_____

_____

_____

_____

Yes, here is the action I will take:

_____

No, here is what I will do instead:

_____

Chapter Eighteen: Decide to Roll with It

Roll with it and don't prejudge. Let's talk about it:

The first thing I want to share with you is "roll with it." There are so many things that happen in your business. You think you're headed in one direction and get tossed a curve ball. Perhaps someone didn't show up for a meeting or someone on your staff decides to move on to another job. That's the one thing about curve-ball-created change: It's constant. If you let the curve balls – the little road blocks or speed bumps you run into, or maybe you call them impediments, disappointments, challenges or whatever you label them – build up, you may get down a bit and it really impedes your effort to move forward.

I'm just like you; I suffer from this. I'll get ticked off or I'll do this, that or the other thing, and I get that feeling and think about it... think about the negativity. The real problem is that a negative and positive thought can't occupy your brain at the same time. When it happens, you can't think about moving your business forward and, at the same time, dwell on the negativity caused by curve balls. You have to roll with different things.

When my daughter, Amanda, was married, the week leading up to the wedding was pretty hectic, and although Stephanie and Amanda did the lion's share of planning, I was very busy with it the week before. On that Wednesday, Amanda approached me with a request: Rather than the typical slow father/daughter dance, she wanted to know if I was game to do something wild and crazy. Admittedly, I was very hesitant, but since I love my daughter to death, I'll do anything for her. It was outside my comfort zone, but I DECIDED to just roll with it.

We improvised. We came up with a few props... very, very last minute stuff. I was also working on my big speech to deliver during the reception. There was a lot going on and a couple of challenges in my business as well. I decided to walk away from the business on Thursday and simply  be in the moment for the wedding and focus on that. Of course, certain things happened, and I just rolled with it. (By the way, you can see our wild and crazy father-daughter dance on my YouTube Channel: https://www.youtube.com/watch?v=4S7AB7iPNfk.)

You need to roll with the challenges in order to grow your business. When a curve ball comes your way, ask what you can learn from it to apply in the future to avoid a repetition of that particular curve ball. If there's really nothing to learn, simply put it in the past and move forward. If you dwell on the challenge or the negativity of the situation, there is no room in your head for positive thoughts about how to grow your business. If you dwell on

DECISION POINT

Accept that curve balls will always come your way. Learn from them or roll with the punches and move forward.

the challenge, you're putting yourself on the road to Squishyville – the awful place where nothing happens. You cannot advance your business when you're there.

Accept the fact that there is nothing but constant change, a few challenges, and different opportunities. Just roll with the changes and challenges and look for ways to convert them to opportunities.

Prejudging

Secondly, DECIDE not to prejudge. I coach many people about the different opportunities that they often don't see in their own businesses, and it seems that there's a lot of prejudging or prequalifying that occurs. It typically runs the gamut when we discuss exploring a new revenue stream, meeting with a potential client, attending a conference or networking at an event that has the potential to gain many new clients. You can prejudge anything.

As I talk about these ideas with different coaching clients, suddenly there's a lot of prejudging that occurs. For example, "Oh, there won't be anybody there for me to meet. That will be a complete waste of time. I talked to that person three years ago, and they had no interest in what I'm offering."

In other words, all of these different preconceived notions are part of a mindset that happens when things get a little harder and you want quicker results. You convince yourself that you are not going to pursue it to see what happens. Your prejudgment of things, events, or people is prohibiting forward progress because you are effectively avoiding a decision. You do not have a valid reason not to pursue it. You're basing a "no" decision on "facts not in evidence." You're basing your decision on your prejudgment rather than keeping an open mind to growth possibilities.

That is not good. Maybe you attend a live event and there turns out to be a crowd of your target audience with higher level decision makers who can truly help you grow your business. Or perhaps you go to a live event filled with a lot of newbies and beginners who aren't your target crowd. But many times, you can't know this for certain in advance. Don't prejudge it. Ultimately, if you meet one or two people who are higher level potential prospects (out of a crowd of newbies or beginners) and one of them becomes a client, I would suspect that going to that event would really pay off for you.

Don't prejudge and don't prequalify these different things. Sure, you have to apply some kind of rationale and critical thought process to your decision. But in the end, don't prejudge the outcome because you never know what's going to happen. You have to do many, many different things. It's very similar to what I coach about marketing: Should I do email marketing, direct response, or printed mail? You do them all to discover which one works the best for your business. Should I do this, that or the other thing? Well, you've got to do a little bit of everything, so you can discover which brings you the greatest ROI.

You can't do one or two things and hope that it's going to move your business forward. DECIDE to test. You've got to go out there and test. If something doesn't work, you can tweak it or choose not to repeat it. That's okay – your decision is based on facts and actual outcomes; your decision is not based on your prejudged expectation of what is going to happen.

Pulling the Ultimate Success Trigger:

❖ *Accept the fact that curve balls and challenges are a part of business and life. Roll with them.*

❖ *You cannot maintain negative and positive thoughts in your head simultaneously. If you dwell on the negativity, you will not have the brain power to move your business forward.*

❖ *When you're thrown a curve ball, figure out what you can learn from it. If there's no applicable lesson, roll with it and decide to move on!*

❖ *Roll with the changes and challenges and look for ways to convert them to opportunities.*

❖ *Never prejudge a situation, person, or event. Prejudging is rarely, if ever, accurate.*

❖ *Decide to test. If something doesn't work, tweak it or choose not to repeat it ONLY AFTER you experience the actual outcome... not your preconceived notion of what might happen.*

DECIDE:

Business… and life… are full of challenges. If you can't learn from them, DECIDE to roll with them and move on. Additionally, prejudging anything rarely turns out to be accurate.

How you will create the mindset to "roll with it" and how you will avoid prejudgment?

Pros:

_____

_____

_____

_____

Cons:

_____

_____

_____

_____

Yes, here is the action I will take:

_____

No, here is what I will do instead:

_____

Chapter Nineteen:
Decide to DECIDE

Throughout this book, I've shared a lot of my own personal demons and 3:00 a.m. moments and what I DECIDED to do as a result of them. These middle of night "holy crap" moments are an integral part of the life of every entrepreneur.

In interviewing some of the members of the Dream Business Mastermind for some of the concepts I've presented in this book, I also asked them each about their 3:00 a.m. moments, what they learned from them, and what they DECIDED to do as a result. There was one great nugget of information after another as we spoke, so I want to share them with you.

Poverty Consciousness

Brad Szollose explained:

"I have whittled down the poverty consciousness that was taught to me as a child and that contributes to my head trash to smaller and smaller pieces, but I still catch myself once in a while having a bit of reversion.

"Poverty consciousness doesn't mean you're poor; it means you place limitations within your consciousness that actually make no sense whatsoever. Long ago, a friend, a Viet Nam Navy vet, was living a joyous life, traveled the world, lived an abundant lifestyle. He wasn't making a lot of money but living this great lifestyle. He obviously wasn't living a poverty consciousness. On the other hand, I've met millionaires who won't hire a nurse to care for a sick loved one because they're counting pennies, stuck in a poverty consciousness without joy, living in misery.

"I have always analyzed this in myself. There was a certain amount of guilt when I became successful... thinking I wasn't supposed to be like this because wealth carried negative connotations. I DECIDED not to live with a poverty consciousness.

It shifts your energy and mindset when you change your thinking and your mindset about the way you are going to live."

Get Out of My Own Way

Dr. Carri Drzyzga shared her 3:00 a.m. moment:

"About six months after I had the revelation about my fear of success, I was reflecting on my year and wasn't happy. Goals didn't get accomplished, and I was still struggling financially and still stuck in the same spot. It hit me that I was the problem. I was getting in my own way. I also realized that I was a bag of excuses and no action. I made the commitment to get out of my own way and put my money where my mouth was. I joined Jim's highest level coaching program, VIP Elite, so that would also put a lot of financial pressure on me. Four months later, my book was off to the publisher, I re-branded, added three new websites, started my blog and podcast, and I finally started my video channel. Taking a long, hard look at myself and realizing that I was the problem made the difference. Ultimately, it was up to me… if this was going to work, I had to step into a zone of uncomfortableness. Now my practice is growing and people are coming from quite a distance, including from across the country, and there are now international patients as well.

"When you become known as the go-to person in your niche, and market it using Jim's Million Dollar Platform, people will seek you out."

Getting Clarity

Dr. Michele Summers Colon said: "There was a moment when I questioned what I REALLY wanted. Once I got clarity about that, it became easy to move forward and get past the doubts.

I know that I'm helping others and being of service while maintaining alignment with my core beliefs and true desires."

Using Skill Sets

Gary George also has 3:00 a.m. moments:

"When financial pressure hits, it's a big motivator for me. There were times when I was very concerned about where the next dollar was coming from. One day I said to myself, 'You need to use all the skill sets you use for your clients for you!' I also realized that it takes the same amount of time to land a big client as a small client.

"I realized that what was holding me back was head trash. I thought these corporations would never do business with a solopreneur like me. But when I finally got up enough gumption to call on them, I realized these guys didn't know as much as I did. They were then glad to bring me in as part of the team.

"A big turning point for me in working with bigger companies was realizing that I'm just as smart as they are. They're regular people.

"When I started working with celebrities, it was also intimidating. But I learned so fast that they're normal, regular people. They would dissociate themselves with fans, and they enjoyed being around people who weren't star-struck and always agreeing with them. Now they tell me that I taught them x, y, and z."

If Not Now...

Susie Miller summed up her 3:00 a.m. realization this way:

"The biggest 3:00 a.m. moment for me was 'If not now, when?' Someday never comes. Do I want to stay the same or go for it? There's a 55-foot high cliff in Hawaii that I'd seen in a movie that the characters jumped off of, and I always wanted to do that. On a vacation there, I climbed up that cliff and realized I'd probably never be in Hawaii again, and asked, 'If not now, when?'

I sucked it up and jumped scared. It became a metaphor in my business and my personal life too: Jumping scared and no more wasting time. I keep a picture of that cliff on my desk."

I love how Susie has pictures on her desk to serve as both reminders and inspiration. Visualization is powerful. For many years, I kept a picture of me driving a rented ski boat (on the left) on my desk. I wanted to be reminded every day of my life-long dream and goal of owning a boat, and last year I made that dream come true. I now have a larger framed picture of my boat sitting on my desk.

Two lessons: If there is something you want and strive for, make sure you "see" it all the time. The constant visualization triggers something in the brain, and your subconscious mind will work to figure out how to make it happen.

Secondly, and the larger point is this: Dreams do come true. Despite many problems, we live in an amazing country where you are free to pursue just about anything you want. If you want a Dream Business and you want to live your dream lifestyle, I believe that you can make it happen. Like me, you can take your small photograph of a "rented" dream and actually create the Dream Business you want. I guarantee you that it will not be easy. No matter how talented you are, your journey will likely be harder than you thought – but in the end, it will be so rewarding.

Remember the lesson I shared about my daughter wanting to join my mastermind program? There is no free lunch and any sort of feeling you have about being entitled to something or that everything will be amazing if you could just win the lottery is useless thinking. Lottery-ticket thinking will slow you down. Believing that there is the possibility of an amazing short cut or windfall will slow you down. It tells your brain, "No worries, we don't have to do 'XYZ' right how – there is an easier way."

The sooner you have your "holy crap" 3:00 a.m. moment, and more importantly, the faster you engage your own talents and abilities and the talents and abilities of other successful people who have blazed the trail ahead of you, the sooner you will create your Dream Business.

There's a great line in the movie "The Pursuit of Happyness" with Will Smith portraying Chris Garner. In this scene, Chris Garnder is talking to his young son and he says, "Don't let anyone tell you that you can't do something – not even me. You got a dream, you got to protect it. People can't do something themselves, they tell you can't do it. If you have a dream, you go get it – period."

I remember a time when my self-esteem and confidence were in tatters, I was broke, heavily in debt and had just fought cancer. That's when I started my first business, and I fought for 12 long months to get my first client.

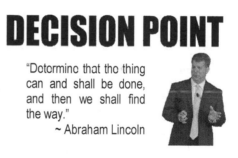

DECISION POINT

"Determine that the thing can and shall be done, and then we shall find the way."
~ Abraham Lincoln

In the meantime, because my kids wanted to have a steady supply of food, in addition to Stephanie working, I took a job stocking shelves at Target. I woke at 4:00 a.m. and stocked shelves with Tide detergent for hours, then drove home and worked on my business. I went to every networking event I could find, sometimes two a night, and then crashed into bed ready for the next 4:00 a.m. alarm. Sometimes when I share that story, someone will ask me, "How did it make you feel from going from corporate executive to starting your own business and yet having to stock shelves at Target?" I tell them that I did what I had to do as a father and a man to help provide for my family.

When I look back on those long days of stress and anxiety with the clarity of hindsight, I realize that taking that job at Target stocking shelves, when I was an entrepreneur, was my first opportunity to prove that I was "all in," and I was willing to invest in my future growth and profitability. Nobody was going to stop me, not even myself.

So I think I'll close this coaching session (I mean book!) with a few ideas for you to think about:

- It's time for you to DECIDE that the time is now.
- It's time for you to DECIDE to jump.
- It's time for you to DECIDE to take out the head trash that is holding you back.
- It's time for you to DECIDE to get clarity about what you want and how you define success.
- It's time for you to DECIDE that you deserve all of the wealth and success that you can muster.
- It's time for you to DECIDE to stop being the impediment to you own success.
- It's time for you to invest in your future growth and profitability.

On the next few pages, if you're ready to grow your Dream Business, I'll share some of the ways that I can help you. You'll see some resources – some free and some worthy of your investment. I'll also share some additional information about my Dream Business Coaching and Mastermind program. As with everything, it is all up to you.

My final question for you is this: If not now, then when?
DECIDE.

About the Contributors

Melanie Benson Strick, America's Leading Small Business Optimizer, helps fast-paced, creative entrepreneurs accelerate their impact and income by making the business they have work ten times better. With over 12 years in corporate America, Melanie specializes in getting creative visionaries focused on their highest payoff opportunities.

Melanie combines her extensive traditional education (she holds a Bachelor's Degree in Business Management and a Master's Degree in Organizational Management) with multiple advanced certifications in Project Management, Results Coaching, Neuro-Linguistic Programming and even a license as a Spiritual Counselor to get her clients past their obstacles and into impacting the world in a fulfilling, and profitable, way.

Melanie speaks for many entrepreneurial audiences across the globe both live and virtually via webinars and telephone-based seminars; has been a regularly featured expert on radio shows and in media publications such as *American Express OPEN Forum*, *Women's Day*, *Parenting Magazine*, *University of Phoenix Alumni Magazine* and *Female Entrepreneur Magazine*.

In addition to multiple business trainings in systems, marketing and advanced success strategies, Melanie is also certified in Neuro-Linguistic Programming (NLP) and Hypnosis, Master NLP Trainer, is a Licensed Spiritual Counselor, a graduate of Coach U, and has an accreditation as an Insights Discovery System™ Facilitator. Melanie also holds a Masters of Arts in Organizational Management and a Bachelor's of Science in Business Management.

www.SuccessConnection.com

Steve Graves, Sr. worked for over 30 years helping hospitals and physicians manage their information needs with Shared Medical Systems. After leaving SMS in 2005, Steve earned his MBA in Organization Management from Eastern University where he and his team developed the foundation for what is now today Play-a-Round Golf. Steve and his wife, Sue, have three grown children and two grandchildren. Steve's son, Steve Jr, works for Play-a-Round Golf.

http://playaroundgolf.net

Brad Szollose is a global business adviser and the foremost expert on Workforce Culture Intelligence…which includes a deep understanding of Millennials. Author of the award-winning, international bestseller Liquid Leadership, Brad is a former C-level executive of a publicly traded company that went from entrepreneurial start-up to IPO within three years. His company K2 Design, became the first Dot Com Agency to go public in an IPO on NASDAQ, experiencing 425% hyper-growth for 5 straight years due in part to a unique management style that won K2 several business awards.

Today, Brad helps smart companies understand just how much technology has transformed a new generation, and how that impacts corporate culture, management interaction, expectations, productivity and sales in The Information Age.

www.liquidleadership.com

Dr. Anthony Weinert is a board certified physician and surgeon of the foot and ankle. He is also the founder and CEO of the Stop Feet Pain Fast Institute, located in Michigan. Dr. Weinert is known for his caring, educating, and his overall concern for patient care and safety. Dr. Weinert prides himself on his holistic approach to foot care. Dr. Weinert served for eight years as the Chief of Podiatric Medicine & Surgery at Henry Ford Bi-county Hospital located in Warren, Michigan. Dr. Weinert has served as team consultant for many high school, college, and professional sports teams in Michigan.

These qualities make Dr. Weinert the go-to expert and recognized authority for many premier national media outlets, including radio, TV, Internet and magazines, when it comes to articles and information on foot care. Dr. Weinert is also a published author of a book on foot and ankle wellness, titled *Stop Feet Pain Fast- A User's Guide to Foot & Ankle Health*. Dr. Weinert is also host of "Happy Feet Radio" which is a radio show dedicated to foot and ankle health wellness. Dr. Weinert believes in the motto "Happy Feet, Happy Life!" Dr. Weinert's life mission is to give back and serve others and to educate others on how to live a healthy and quality filled life.

www.stopfeetpainfast.com

Susie Albert Miller, MA, MDiv is The Better Relationship Coach™. As a therapist/coach, Susie's passion is to help people have better relationships with each other, themselves, and God. For over 20 years, Susie has helped people reduce stress, communicate better, and grow deeper in their faith. If you want to stop beating yourself up, increase your self-confidence, understand how God loves you; or if you are tired of feeling lonely, misunderstood or frustrated with your spouse, kids, or coworkers, Susie is here to help!

Susie is a cancer survivor, has overcome numerous health challenges and difficult life experiences. She believes faith, perseverance, and grace are key to moving from just surviving to thriving in life. Her personal life has been referred to as a Shakespearean tragedy, but she's known for looking at life as a "possibilitarian"! She and her husband John have been married for 32 years. They have three adult children, who bring them joy, laughter and more than a few wrinkles! Susie loves dark chocolate, great shoes and lingering conversations.

www.susiemiller.com

Dr. Michele Summers Colon, a physician, surgeon, certified yoga teacher, author and overall health and wellness expert, is known as The Holistic Podiatrist of Southern California and has been interviewed and quoted in many prominent publications. One of Dr. Michele's greatest strengths is her ability to combine the best of Eastern and Western medicine to treat the whole patient and create individualized treatment plans, yoga sequences, and meal plans for her clients and patients. She believes that food is medicine and that yoga, Ayurveda, and meditation are the keys to perfect health. She has even created a shoe company for women called 34 Minutes to alleviate the pain associated with women's footwear. A Los Angeles based doctor and yoga teacher, Dr. Michele has been featured in various print and online publications, including *USA Today, US News & World Report, Sole Sisters, Beauty Fashion & War, Career 100: On Becoming a Podiatrist, Made Woman Magazine*, and others.

www.elmontefootdoctor.com ~ www.34minutesshoes.com

Dr. Carri Drzyzga DC, ND, is known as "The Functional Medicine Doc" – the go-to expert on finding the root causes of health problems, so you can feel normal again. She is a chiropractor and naturopathic doctor, host of the popular podcast "The Functional Medicine Radio Show", and author of the hit book *Reclaim Your Energy and Feel Normal Again! Fixing the Root Cause of Your Fatigue with Natural Treatments*. Her newest program is Entrepreneurial Fatigue: How to Fuel Your Brain & Body for Entrepreneurial Success. Her private practice is Functional Medicine Ontario located in Ottawa, Ontario. To learn more about Dr. Carri go to www.DrCarri.com.

Kelly Roach is a Business Growth Catalyst and has helped hundreds of individuals rapidly grow their businesses and multiply their incomes. Kelly teaches business owners proven and profitable strategies to skyrocket their sales, increase their profits and become a true industry leader. By teaching business leaders how to implement strategy and systems in their business, Kelly takes the guess work out of creating rapid, sustainable growth without compromising your quality of life.
www.kellyroachcoaching.com

About the Contributors

About the Author – Jim

Learn More About Jim:

Jim's other books:

The Magic of Newsletter Marketing – The Secret to More Profits and Customers for Life

Stick Like Glue – How to Create an Everlasting Bond with Your Customers So They Stay Longer, Spend More, and Refer More!

The Fastest Way to Higher Profits – 19 Immediate Profit-Enhancing Strategies You Can Use Today

It's Okay to Be Scared – But Never Give Up (with Martin Howey)

Stop Waiting For It to Get Easier – Create Your Dream Business Now!

Get Jim's Books At
http://www.SuccessAdvantagePublishing.com

Check out Jim's wildly popular Smart Marketing and Business Building Programs:

No Hassle Newsletters – www.NoHassleNewsletters.com

No Hassle Social Media – www.NoHassleSocialMedia.com

Newsletter Guru TV – www.NewsletterGuru.TV

Stick Like Glue Radio – www.GetJimPalmer.com

Jim's Concierge Print and Mail on Demand Program – www.newsletterprintingservice.com

Double My Retention – www.DoubleMyRetention.com

How to Sell From The Stage Like a Pro – www.howtosellfromthestage.com/

Custom Article Generator – www.customarticlegenerator.com

No Hassle Inforgraphics – www.nohassleinfographics.com

Dream Business Mastermind and Coaching – www.DreamBizCoaching.com

Dream Business Academy – www.DreamBizAcademy.com

The Magnetic Attraction and Retention System (MARS Training Program) – www.MarsTrainingProgram.com

Interested in interviewing Jim? Visit www.GetJimPalmer.com or contact Jessica@InterviewConnections.com

About Jim

Jim Palmer is a marketing and business-building expert and in demand coach. He is the founder of the Dream Business Academy and Dream Business Coaching and Mastermind Program. Jim is the host of Newsletter Guru TV, the hit weekly web TV show watched by thousands of entrepreneurs and small business owners, and he is also the host Stick Like Glue Radio, a weekly podcast based on Jim's unique brand of smart marketing and business-building strategies.

Jim is best known internationally as "The Newsletter Guru" and creator of No Hassle Newsletters, the ultimate "done-for-you" newsletter marketing program used by hundreds of clients in nine countries.

Jim is the acclaimed author of:

The Magic of Newsletter Marketing – The Secret to More Profits and Customers for Life

Stick Like Glue – How to Create an Everlasting Bond With Your Customers So They Spend More, Stay Longer, and Refer More

The Fastest Way to Higher Profits – 19 Immediate Profit-Enhancing Strategies You Can Use Today

It's Okay To Be Scared – But Don't Give Up – A book of hope and inspiration for life and business

Stop Waiting for It to Get Easier – Create Your Dream Business Now!

Jim was also privileged to be a featured expert in *The Ultimate Success Secret; Dream, Inc.; ROI Marketing Secrets Revealed; The Barefoot Executive;* and *Boomers in Business.*

Jim speaks and gives interviews on such topics as newsletter marketing, client retention, entrepreneurial success, the fastest way to higher profits, how to use social media marketing, and how to achieve maximum success in business.

Jim is a cancer survivor, has been married for 34 years, has four grown children and a grandson. He lives in Chester County, Pennsylvania with his wife, Stephanie, their cat, Linus, and Toby, the marketing dog. Jim and Stephanie love to kayak, travel, and spend time with their family.

Connect with Jim on Facebook, Twitter, Google+, LinkedIn®, and tune into his web TV show.

For more resources and information on Jim, his blog, and his companies, visit www.GetJimPalmer.com.

Subscribe to Jim's free weekly newsletter, "More Profits and Customers for Life," at www.GetJimPalmer.com.

DECIDE & SAVE $100!

If you've decided that "slow to no growth" is no longer an acceptable option and are finally ready to accelerate the growth and profitability of your business, then I invite you to join me and a small group of entrepreneurs at my next Dream Business Academy. And because you've already invested in yourself by reading this book, I'd like to reward you with a $100 discount! To claim your $100 discount, simply go to www.DreamBizAcadmey.com and when you register, enter the coupon code: **DECIDE.**

NOTE: Seating at Dream Business Academy is limited by design. We are currently running two events a year, one in spring and one in the fall. If you try to register and the current event is sold out, then please email guru@thenewsletterguru.com and ask to be put on the waiting list and also be notified when the next event is scheduled.

If you've DECIDED that slow-to-no growth is no longer an acceptable option for your business, then consider applying for Jim's Dream Business Mastermind and Coaching Program.

What is a Dream Business?
A Dream Business:

- Grows even during a crappy economy
- Has multiple streams of revenue
- Becomes an asset for worry-free retirement
- Is always firing on all cylinders
- Is fun to operate
- Provides the lifestyle you want
- Allows you to give back and make a difference in the lives of others

What Makes Jim Palmer's Dream Business Coaching and Mastermind Group Unique?

- This group is not for tire-kickers.
- Everyone in the group has been meticulously vetted before approval.
- All members come to the group prepared to give as much as they look to receive.
- Members participate in monthly group mastermind calls and get a private 1:1 monthly coaching call with Jim.
- Depending on your level, members have additional access to Jim between monthly calls.
- Every member makes a one-year commitment to the group and themselves.
- The Dream Business Private Facebook group is often a "port in the storm" for busy entrepreneurs building their Dream Businesses. Members regularly interact, post questions, success stories, and get feedback, motivation and moral support from each other.

Is this Coaching Program Right For You?

- If you're at the point in your business where you finally decide that slow-to-no growth is no longer an acceptable option.
- If you want to play a bigger game and are ready to experience real growth in your business.
- If you're ready to be part of an elite group of forward-thinking and action-oriented entrepreneurs.
- If you're ready to invest in your future growth and profitability.
- If you're open to new ideas and perhaps changing direction to achieve your Dream Business.
- If you're ready to create wealth instead of simply selling more of what you currently offer.
- If you answered yes to any of the above questions, then review the three Dream Business Coaching Options and decide how fast and how far you want to grow, and apply today!

If you answer yes, then apply today at www.DreamBizCoaching.com!

Get My Free Marketing App!

My free marketing app is getting rave reviews and has been downloaded over 8000 times! The vast majority of the content, what I often refer to as my Smart Marketing and Business Building Advice,™ is free and you can use much of it to help build your business! It is available for both Android and I-Phone – just search 'Jim Palmer' or 'Smart Marketing' and get yours today!

Made in the USA
Charleston, SC
27 March 2015